# THE REVIEWS

❞ The BoltBros have written an inspiring book full of clear and energetic wisdom about how to create a life rather than have it happen to you. This is Rage Against The Machine meets Dave Ramsey at its finest! (You just don't see that combo often) This should be required reading for every high schooler-or college student-or anybody working a job they don't enjoy. There ought to be stacks of this book in the of                                         d academic advisors. T                                          g in how they show w                                          d generosity looks like.

Pastor, Inn
bes

❞ Not just another self-help book. Funny, entertaining and brilliant! A must-read.

### Chip Conley
*New York Times* best selling author of *Emotional Equations: Simple Truths for Creating Happiness + Success*

★     ★     ★

❞ Breaking Out of A Broken System is everything you want in a great book. It's creative, thoughtful, informative, fun to look at, easy-to-read, and written with character, wit, intelligence and humor. As you follow the journals of these two wildly successful brothers, you'll not only feel like you're in the conversation with them, you'll more than likely discover – as they did – you have the power to change the world.

### Alliso
Author of *Packing Light: Thou                                 gage*

D1057307

**"** As a father of five, I've really enjoyed reading this book! It has not only helped me to learn some valuable life lessons and tips, it has also encouraged me in new ways to inspire my children! A GREAT book about lessons learned from loving parents that help their children to live more productive lives and to chase their dreams!

**Mac Powell**
Vocalist for Third Day

★    ★    ★

**"** This book is a cup of cool water on a long run. Seth and Chandler don't give you a map for success in this book, they let us eavesdrop on a great conversation they're having about what they've learned.

**Bob Goff**
*New York Times* best selling author of *Love Does*

★    ★    ★

**"** Seth and Chandler Bolt's Breaking Out of a Broken System is filled with incredible insight and inspiration. Humble roots run deep and provide the strength for these brothers to fulfill their dreams of becoming a rock star and successful entrepreneur. Their stories and observations, presented in a clever dual perspective format, use warmth and wit to share life lessons with sincerity and encouragement.

**Tim Taylor**
Co-founder, *America Succeeds*

★    ★    ★

**"** This practical guide of success secrets comes from an unexpected source: two brothers who have been tremendously successful in two completely different paths. This book is humble, personable, useful and delightfully inspiring.

**Rory Vaden**
Co-founder of Southwestern Consulting and *New York Times* best selling author of *Take the Stairs*

# Breaking Out of a Broken System

© 2014 Seth Bolt and Chandler Bolt

ISBN-13: 978-1494243395
ISBN-10: 1494243393

BoltBros Publishing | www.boltbros.com
For orders, please email: breakingoutbooks@gmail.com

# DOWNLOAD THE AUDIOBOOK!

Are you an audiobook person? Just to say thanks for buying our book, we'd like to give you the audiobook 100% FREE!

## Go to BoltBros.com/Audiobook to download it!

BOLT BROS

# THAT DESERVES REPEATING ... AND TWEETING!

# 1 BOOK

# =

# 1 LIFE

**SOLD!**

**SAVED!**

**#1BOOK1LIFE**

## TWEET

Help us save 10,000 people from dying of malaria this year!
One mosquito bite - something so small yet so lethal - can end a life.
One book sale - something so small yet so powerful - can save that
life. Your purchase of this book bought one life-saving malaria pill!
Spread the word! One tweet can make a BIG difference!

—————— **#1BOOK1LIFE** ——————

# THE CHARACTERS

Seth is a successful musician, Chandler a successful entrepreneur. Born a decade apart, they both attribute their success in art and business to the "roadmap" their parents handed down to them: essentially, a life map crisscrossed with lessons about faith, planning, hard work, determination, and giving to others.

# THE DEDICATION

Our parents grew up in two neighboring small towns in rural South Carolina, both the children of hardworking but poor parents. They married and set up house with little more than the wedding gifts they received. They both worked full-time, learned the value of a dollar, and lived paycheck-to-paycheck. With little savings to their credit, they learned how to scrimp and scrape to get by, taking money saving measures like planting their own garden and canning their own produce when the harvest came in (even though they weren't farmers by trade.)

They wanted something more than "getting by" for their children. Using their experiences — triumphs and mistakes, beliefs handed down by their parents, as well as ideas of their own — they created a map to success. They put the plan into action and carried it out over the days and weeks of our childhoods, year in and year out. Since the two of us grew up a decade apart, they spent the better part of 25 years pouring their lives, their lessons, and their aspirations for us into our minds.

We hated it.

We didn't appreciate the early morning wake-ups, the insistence on doing things a certain way, the focus on full effort and attention. It looked an awful lot like work, and nothing like the fun our friends were having watching cartoons.

But as we both went out into the world, leaving our parents' home, we realized a funny thing had happened. Then we had this super important phone call.

# THE CALL...

My brother Chandler had just received the coveted Entrepreneur of the Year Award from a national company. I was calling not only to congratulate him for that, but to ask him about his recent meeting with the company. They flew him to their headquarters to wine and dine him, and ultimately BEG him to sign a lucrative contract so that he would teach the rest of their staff "the secret of his success."

PORTLAND, OR

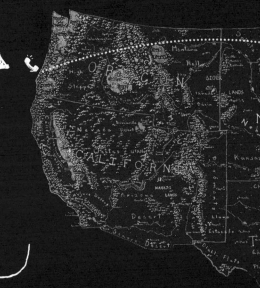

And why wouldn't they? He earned OVER A HUNDRED THOUSAND DOLLARS in one summer break. (He's an 18 year old "kid" for crying out loud!) Chandler was their newest hire, started at the very bottom, and in two and a half months had broken every sales record imaginable.

# ...THAT CHANGED EVERYTHING

Seth had called to congratulate me on my recent Entrepreneur of the Year Award, but I was more interested in hearing about the tour he was on. Seth is my older brother and I've watched with envy, for the past decade, as his band has grown to the international success they have today. They've toured across the US & Europe, played shows for crowds of over 100,000 people, been on every Late show possible, and they're continuing to grow. As a producer, he's also worked with some extremely talented artists and is helping some of the best up-and-coming artists get their start in the industry. He's getting to do what I would kill to be able to do; travel and play music!! At 28, he's experienced and achieved more than most people will their entire lives.

CHARLESTON, SC

Basically, don't do anything too crazy or out of the ordinary.

Well, obviously there's so much more to life than that! We all know that, and yet so many of us still follow the same beaten path, even though our unlived life is beckoning us from the road less traveled. We work our whole lives for a few years of retirement because that's the way the system works, right? Do we really have a choice? After college, our first marching orders for that system is a steep mountain of debt to climb ($27,500 on average) with little to no wiggle room to blaze our own trail or explore the outliers and "what ifs" we encounter along the way.

We get in line because that's what we've been equipped to do. We follow the tried and true path because we were never taught the necessary street smarts needed to forge a different path. We aren't taught these street smarts in school, and sadly most people aren't taught them at home either.

We (Seth & Chandler) were equipped with these "street smarts" through the teachings of our parents, who learned these lessons the hard way. We've interviewed them about the empowering lessons that they taught us and we'll be passing them along in this book.

Our goal is to inspire, inform, and empower people to accomplish the big dreams, spoken and unspoken alike, and avoid the systematic traps that derail most people from their true purpose. We believe in challenging the status quo. Each of us has a voice, a song, and a purpose.

There is strength and the potential for greatness inside of you, and you deserve the true happiness that comes from discovering, chasing, and living your purpose.

Finally ... Christmas break is here!

12/20/12 - 10:13 pm: We meet in our hometown, Walhalla, SC. Our parents are out of town. We have nothing to write on.

We buy black construction paper, silver sharpies, and pencils without erasers.

10:17 pm: ... celebrate with donuts in a vacant gravel parking lot on the way home. We're doing this! One book. Seven days. It will be done!

**10:21 pm:** We're home now. Getting set up. "Hey ... let's do this!"

We clink our cell phones together like wine glasses, power them off, and put them in a drawer, promising to take them out only for pictures.

After a few brainstorming exercises, we really hit our stride. While making a list of the most important things that Mom and Dad did for us, Seth writes down "taught us how to break out of a broken system," and Chandler says, "That's it, that's our title!" We map out our writing schedule for the week, decide on our chapter topics and call it a night.

# THE WAY THIS BOOK WORKS

**Editor's Note:** Seth's story was written on black paper. Chandler's story was written on white paper. This design element is consistent throughout the book. Two different sides of the stories join together to provide one radically different experience.

# TO READ SETH'S 7 DAY JOURNAL, START HERE

To read Chandler's journal go to page CB-1 for an entirely different, yet practical perspective!

# SETH'S
# SIDE OF THE STORIES

# DAY 1
## YOUR MINDSET

# CHALLENGING THE STATUS QUO

The artistic rebellion of reaching higher
and confronting normality

*12/21/12 - 10:54 am*

*I'm gonna do my best to narrate this crazy one-week brotherly book-writing journey by starting each chapter with what's happening around me and by typing my thoughts in italics along the way. We'll be traveling quite a bit, so I'll try my best to make it feel like you're right here with us! Music is a huge part of my life, so I've created a Spotify playlist for this week's journey that's full of music that inspires me. I'll tell you the song I'm listening to at the beginning of each chapter if you want to listen along with me. Here we go!*
*(Go to www.sethbolt.me for the link.)*

*Chandler and I have the house to ourselves. Mom and Dad are vacationing down on Edisto Island, South Carolina. It feels very different waking up in my parents' house without them here, but it's making it easier for Chandler and me to talk and write about them freely.*

*Earlier this morning we created a writing map that will give us a chance to share the most important stories and lessons of our youth. We needed a chalkboard or a dry erase board but we didn't have one. I thought it might be cool to write everything on the walls in one of our old bedrooms, but Chandler, being the mama's boy that he is, wouldn't let me. He was afraid Mom might disown us or hyperventilate upon discovering that her boys graffitied her walls with king size Sharpies. So improvising, we created a dry erase board using craft paper! It doesn't erase, so I said to Chandler "We'll have to be sure of ourselves." Little brother quickly jabbed back, "That won't be hard for you." Funny. I decided not to punch him yet.*

*Punching Chandler is something I was never allowed to do growing up. Being ten years older, I was always much, much, much stronger, and it just wouldn't have been a fair fight. This week might be my chance if he doesn't stow that sass.*

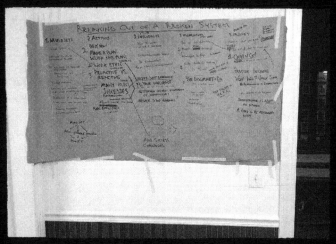

HERE IT IS! WE'RE CALLING IT THE "BIG BOARD"

 *"Bulls On Parade" by Rage Against The Machine*

──────────────────────────────→

# REBELLION IS A GOOD THING

### "STATUS QUO"
[ˈstātəs ˈkwō, ˈstatəs]
*noun* (usu. the status quo): the existing state of affairs

## Think about these people:

| | | |
|---|---|---|
| Abraham Lincoln | Rosa Parks | Harriet Tubman |
| Leonardo Da Vinci | Thomas Edison | Wright Brothers |
| Ludwig van Beethoven | Chuck Berry | Kurt Cobain |
| William Wallace | Mohandas Gandhi | Martin Luther King Jr. |
| Jesus Christ | Florence Nightingale | Mother Theresa |
| Amelia Earhart | Jackie Robinson | Walt Disney |
| Henry David Thoreau | Benjamin Franklin | Thomas Paine |

Different centuries ... different countries ... different endeavors ... but they all had one thing in common: They ignored the prevailing wisdom and charted their own path. They were willing to break the rules. They believed that they knew the right path to take and they didn't let convention, negativity, or resistance from others stop them.

**Rebellious** is a label given to innovators *before* they succeed. After they succeed, they are given a new label: **hero**.

These people each made a tremendous mark on the world. Their names are well-known because their marks on history have made them famous. Countless other people do the same thing in their everyday lives and achieve great things, even though you may never have heard of them. They are changing the world, living their dreams, and becoming heroes in their own right — and so can you.

---

"When you realize that life as we know it was just made up by a bunch of people no smarter than you, you'll realize that you have the power to change it."
- Steve Jobs

---

We are all capable of changing the world! Why don't we?

To CHANGE the world, you have to rebel. You have to INTENTIONALLY question the "rules" and expectations that society imposes, and ask whether they help or hinder you. You have to be willing to buck the system where it doesn't support your goals.

"Going along with the crowd" was something my mama always discouraged. Lucky for her, following the crowd was never something I was interested in doing. I've always celebrated individuality, so I guess it shouldn't have surprised (or upset) me that my Senior Superlative in high school was "Most Individual."

I remember being bummed because that was the "weirdo award," but my imaginary friend reassured me that thinking differently is what allows me to create art that people can enjoy. It's different. I'm different. It's okay to be different.

"Why fit in when you were born to stand out?"
- Dr. Seuss

# FITTING IN IS OVERRATED

Regardless of where you're coming from, you have to be doggedly determined to do what you believe you were meant to do. Some people are born great, some people are taught how to be great by their parents, and some people learn to grab greatness by the bootstraps. Those in the last group start at a disadvantage because they are not born into or taught greatness — they have to find it with their own efforts. They have to seek wisdom from external sources and every place imaginable and know in their hearts not how they'll get there, but simply how badly they want it.

What do you believe you are meant to do with your life? And to better fulfill your life's purpose, where do you need to jump off the bandwagon? What rules do you need to break? Sometimes the standard procedure isn't what's best for you and your goals. Don't get in line, do your own thing!

Are you doing work every day that's related to what you love most in life? Do you have a passion so fulfilling that you would do it for free?

# CHALLENGE THE
# FINANCIAL STATUS QUO

What does it mean to have a "normal" amount of debt in America these days? According to The Federal Reserve, the average person has $27,750 in student loan debt; $4,100 in credit card debt; and $95,000 in mortgage debt for a house. Why does being "normal" require so much automatic debt??

We are led to believe that everybody needs a college education, whether it supports their goals and dreams or not, and that you should borrow huge sums of money for that degree — even if you have no clue how you'll pay those loans back. We are encouraged to rack up huge credit card debt. And many of us are seduced into thinking we can have a house beyond our current means, sooner than we can afford it.

To me, that is a systematic approach to tricking people into being STUCK! That's broken!

How are you supposed to live your dreams, do work you love, travel the world, and be fulfilled if you're flat broke when you start your adult life?

# YOU DEFINE YOUR OWN NORMAL

Your normal can be anything you want it to be!

What if you:

★ ... could travel to Africa and Latin America several times a year to build hospitals or to give life-saving medical care?

★ ... were able to spend as much time as you like on a special hobby or passion in your life - something that is not connected to your daily work but that brings you happiness?

★ ... could start a charity to support a cause you really care about, and fund its first 3 years without going into debt yourself?

★ ... were able, every year, to go on a 10-day ski trip plus spend a few weeks of summer at a beautiful lake house?

What do you want your "normal" to be? Do you want it to look a lot different than the "normal" you see around you? The simple fact that you're reading this book probably means that you're hungry to break out of mediocrity. And the love that you have for your art and the dreams you hold close to your heart are beautiful things that deserve your chase. The world needs you and your unique ideas. The greatness you're capable of is worth the work.

# BREAKING OUT!

★ If you had no financial limits, what are two things you'd like to do for yourself and two things you'd like to do for others?

★ ★ ★

## ∾ There is strength in you ∾

# LIMITING BELIEFS VS. EMPOWERING BELIEFS

### Life-hacking your demons

→

*12/21/12 - 1:30 pm - OUR FIRST CALL TO AN EDITOR*
*Chandler just called a professional editor to make sure that our idea for the formatting and layout of this book was even feasible. I got out my phone and started recording the call for reference purposes. We were shot down with immediate resistance. Hear it on my website www.sethbolt.me*

*Chandler: "One side's white with black text, the other side's black with white text."*
*Editor: "I think that's crazy. I'll tell you right now — I think you're out of your mind for doing that. No one's gonna read a book that's got white text on a black background."*

*Wow. So, my idea is crazy, I'm out of my mind for thinking it, and no one is going to read my book. I guess I should just quit.*

*This guy is an established gate-keeper for the book industry, but I don't care. He gave up on creating art a long time ago — on the call he went so far as to tell us the most profitable font to use — what a sell-out! Click.*

*Call me crazy, but I feel motivated by hearing that our idea is crazy.*

*p.s. Tell your friends about this book because it's my new goal in life to prove this guy wrong.*

*p.p.s. Gatekeepers everywhere, pull yourself out of the rut! Just because you've been profitable selling one particular font or playing one type of song on your radio station doesn't mean your audience wants the same thing over and over!*

 *"Have Love, Will Travel" by The Black Keys*

"I think I can. I think I can."
- The little engine that DID

*Beliefs are your rudder*

# WHAT'S STEERING YOU?

The subconscious is a powerful thing. It's the rudder under the boat. You can't see it at work, but you can bet your life vest it's gonna determine where you set your anchor!

# LIES

90% of a child's brain develops during the first three years of childhood. It's taking in information as quickly as possible and writing it on the walls of your skull. If your parents say it, then it must be true, right?

My granny Bolt had TWELVE brothers and sisters! I'll never forget her response when I asked her, "Granny, why did you have so many brothers and sisters?!"

*"Back then, people believed that as long as a woman was breastfeeding, she couldn't get pregnant!"*

Okay, so maybe that knowledge was present in other parts of the world but it hadn't made its way to the hills of South Carolina. The point is, whether they're fundamentally true or fundamentally flawed, your beliefs are the most powerful guiding force inside of you. If you believe something that is flawed, your ship can be taken off course. In order to get back on course, you must examine your rudder. It never hurts to inspect your beliefs from time to time. As we take a look at Limiting Beliefs and empowering beliefs, think about what's steering you.

# LIMITING BELIEFS

Your beliefs are subconsciously steering the decisions you make each day. Limiting Beliefs discourage you from taking positive action and sometimes encourage negative actions. They'll remind you of the time you introduced yourself to a new group of people at a party and they laughed at you because you had Oreos in your teeth, and the clever thing you thought to say totally bombed. Limiting Beliefs — and we all have them — keep us from taking chances and realizing our full potential. Many times we don't realize they are even there because we've made broad generalizations about ourselves like "I'm just not a people person" — which makes it easy to justify not taking a chance on meeting someone great because we're afraid of being rejected. That's broken.

---

"Fear's a powerful thing, babe."
- Bruce Springsteen, "Devils and Dust"

---

Kids are fearless — they know no limitations. Think about the child version of yourself and how he or she could do anything, yet the older version of yourself is boxed in by "realistic" or "safe" boundaries. It's likely the tablespoons of "guidance" you were given growing up were one part wisdom, one part fear.

*"Stop climbing! You're gonna fall and hurt yourself!"*

*"Put on a jacket. You're gonna catch cold."*

*"What will people think?"*

It's safe to say that by the time you're in high school, you've be
to be afraid of a lot of things. You've also encountered failure fi
Maybe some of those failures seemed to confirm your limiting ⸻eliefs.
Maybe you didn't make the cut for the basketball team and you thought,
"Well, I knew I wouldn't make it. I was stupid for even trying."

Failure is inevitable. It doesn't mean all of the worst things you think
about yourself are true! Don't be afraid of it! Never stop trying new
things! Just because you fail at one thing doesn't mean that you can't
use your other talents to be successful.

Fear of failure and fear of rejection are two of the most common
Limiting Beliefs. Each has the power to destructively change the
way you think and behave. These negative beliefs limit your positive
potential!

From time to time, we need to un-learn some stuff. If you can un-learn
your Limiting Beliefs and replace them with empowering beliefs, your
potential will skyrocket!

ALL of your failure is in the past! It doesn't define you unless you let
it. In most cases, you and maybe a small handful of people are the only
ones who know you failed. Shake it off! Welcome back the fearlessness
you had as a child. Keep climbing! Challenge yourself to try new things!
Don't "protect" yourself from failure by not taking chances.

My little secret for protecting my pride is laughing at my failures. I
laugh right along with everyone else who's watching and say, "I've got
a lot of crazy ideas and by God, I'm gonna try 'em all. Not livin' is dyin'
already. I'm goin' for it!" Your friends and family will probably still
belly laugh when one of your big ideas goes awry, but quietly they
will respect and envy your fearlessness.

# EMPOWERING BELIEFS

Empowering beliefs, on the other hand, encourage you and propel you. They accelerate you towards your destinations and dreams. When you see a person you want to introduce yourself to, those beliefs tell you to put on that beautiful smile and go for it!

Empowering beliefs affirm your effort and enable you to achieve your goals. Empowering beliefs are positive thoughts that multiply the joy in your life and springboard your actions toward success.

**Consider these kinds of positive, powerful thoughts**

★ My past does not determine my future.
★ Getting where I want to go will be tough, but I'm tougher.
★ I'm here for a reason.
★ There's no such thing as failure — only feedback.
★ I am going to succeed, even if I don't yet know exactly how.
★ I'm going to need help — and there are people who will help me.
★ I'm not going to be driven by my fears, but by my intentions.
★ I'm my own single greatest resource.

---

"Whether you think you can
or you think you can't, either way you're right."
- Henry Ford

---

| Limiting Belief | Empowering Belief |
|---|---|
| I'm Nobody Special | I add value to the world |
| I'm Not an Author | I have a unique Perspective! |
| The Rules are the rules | Anything is Possible! |
| I'm Damaged Goods | I'm worthy of love! |
| Other people are better than me | I have what it takes to thrive! |
| I am too shy, young, weak, Poor, Unlucky | I Am destined for Success! |

# BREAKING OUT!

Reversing Limiting Beliefs — Turning Limiting Beliefs into empowering ones takes some practice. I've given you a few examples below. You can use these or identify some of your own that might be limiting your potential. If you choose your own, REVERSE that belief. Turn the negative thought into a positive one. Transform the limiting belief into an empowering one! Remember what this feels like so that the next time you feel yourself listening to a limiting belief, you can reverse it and empower yourself to succeed.

| LIMITING BELIEF | EMPOWERING BELIEF |
|---|---|
| I'm not good at anything. | My skillset may not be conventional, but the world needs me and I can do anything I put my mind to! |
| I've made too many mistakes to be able to start over. | My past doesn't determine my future. Today is a new day and a new me. |
| I'll never have enough money to reach my dreams. | Anything is possible if I work hard. I can be the rags-to-riches story that my grandchildren tell their children one day! |
| There's nothing really special about me. | Life isn't about finding yourself, it's about creating yourself. |

★ What are some of your personal Limiting Beliefs and how can you change them into empowering beliefs?

★     ★     ★

∽ There is strength in your beliefs ∾

# UNLOCKING POTENTIAL

### The secrets of my strength coaches

*12/21/12 - 4:00pm*
*I can't believe we've finished two chapters already or that we're using my old alarm clock to keep us working on the same pace! We're taking 10 minutes to privately brainstorm for each chapter, then 10 minutes to make an outline, then 90 minutes to write. Then Chandler is "giving me" a 10-minute break. Which means we are on pace to write one chapter every two hours. I think it says something about my brain that when I'm told to write a story, I draw a picture.*

**"** *Chandler: "Why are you drawing? You're supposed to be writing."*
*Seth: "A picture says a thousand words, man."*
*Chandler: "Dude, you're wasting time."*
*Seth: "Will you just let me be me?"*
*Chandler: "Stick drawings?"*
*Seth: "I happen to like stick drawings."*

*We could not be more different.*

 *"Breathe" by The Brilliance*

# WHAT IF YOU COULD DO ANYTHING?

YOU CAN

# IMAGINE THE POSSIBILITIES

Kids have wild, limitless imaginations. If you're a kid, every day is a new adventure that starts with a dream. One day you might be a pirate looking for treasure, and the next day you're a husband and have three kids (*because the girls roped you into playing house*). Every imagination time begins with one thought: What do I wanna be today? Then, like the little genius that you are, you walk around in those shoes and see what it feels like to be just that. Kids dream, and then they wrap both hands around that dream.

When's the last time you wrapped both hands around your dreams or even envisioned what it might feel like to wake up tomorrow to a life free of your current limitations? Imagination time shouldn't end with childhood. Take the time to let your imagination ask questions like:

*"If I could travel anywhere, where would I go?"*

*"What if I had a magic wand that could radically improve someone's life and that of everyone around them?"*

*"What if I could do anything?"*

It doesn't matter if the questions or the answers seem silly or unrealistic. All the things you dream about doing will shine a light on all the things you shouldn't be. When you "come back to reality," you'll be more aware of the parts of your reality that stand in the way of the life you imagine. Imagination time isn't a waste of time; it keeps you from wasting time. And it would save some people from a lifetime of "chugging along" at a job or in a town that's nothing like the life they want.

---

"Your past is not your potential. In any hour you can choose to liberate the future."
- Marilyn Ferguson

---

"That which doesn't kill me, makes me stronger."
- Nietzsche

# GET A STRENGTH COACH

I'm not much of a weight lifter. And by "not much" of one, I mean I don't lift weights ever. I don't know if it's the relentless Top 40 music, the armpit smell, or the "tough" guys with big arms and little legs, but I've never been motivated to go to the gym. Nevertheless, several years ago I bought a gym membership. I considered it a huge waste of money ... up until the day I saw a poster on the locker room wall, which read:

*"3 months with a personal trainer produces more results than 1 year by yourself."*

I signed up for a personal trainer and I can tell you now that the poster was not lying. As soon as I had someone in my face, yelling, "COME ON! GO! YOU GOT THIS! DO IT!" I forgot about the rap music, the locker room smell, and the much stronger dudes around watching me lift, and I discovered again that I was capable of way more than my unmotivated self was giving me credit for.

When I'm not on the road with NEEDTOBREATHE, I'm a music producer for other artists. I'm like a personal trainer for their songs, so it's my job to help whip them into shape. We challenge and often strengthen all of the song's core elements, the lyrics, the vocal performance, and the musical composition. Sometimes it's exhausting, but after all the work is done, the difference is very noticeable and we're all glad we put in the effort.

The same can be said for my band. We always use a producer or ask for some kind of outside help because inevitably, other people are a better mirror.

Who's pushing you?? Who's strengthening you? Muscles grow only after being challenged and broken down. Your rate of growth will skyrocket when you seek out wise people and ask them to strengthen you. It's no secret. WE ALL *NEED* TO BE CHALLENGED! Welcome it.

Continuous effort and empowering beliefs will take you to the moon and back. Pushing the limits of your current boundaries will unlock all of your potential. Unlocking your potential doesn't require mystical "witchcraftery" or a magic skeleton key. It's the result of determination and continuous effort. Your potential is your capacity for future success.

As you unlock your potential, beautiful things begin to happen: your success begins to empower your beliefs; small problems are no longer insurmountable; medium size dreams don't seem out of reach; and your capacity for success grows! You feel enabled and empowered to reach higher. Continuous effort and determination take you there!

To finish the boat analogy, if beliefs are the rudder, steering your boat and determining your direction, continuous effort and determination are the engine and the propellers.

---

"Continuous effort – not strength or intelligence – is the key to unlocking our potential."
- Liane Cordes

---

# THE TALENT
# OF DETERMINATION

Determination is a total game changer. When I played youth league basketball, my mom was kind enough to give me an angle that helped me overcome my shortcomings and add value to the team. She said, "You don't need muscle to hustle! Your team has talent, but nobody rebounds or hustles to gain possession when the ball is loose. Your good shooters can't score if your team doesn't have possession of the ball. You can be that player and help your team win. Be aggressive out there. Hands up on defense. Hustle! Hustle! Hustle!" I wasn't the fastest or the best shooter but I was determined to get every rebound and every loose ball. I wanted to win, so I hustled. It earned me a starting spot.

I didn't realize it at the time but my mom was teaching me a much larger life lesson: you don't have to be at the top of your class to be successful; you can do a lot with a little. My potential on the basketball court was realized when I became determined to do more with the scraps than anyone else. The coach knew that we had a better chance of winning if I was in the game because I could get the ball into the hands of the players with "real" talent!

Determination is a different talent than speed and strength. Determination by definition is a firmness of purpose used to achieve a goal *after you understand your goal.* But few people emphasize using determination to *discover* your goal! Determination is a valuable mindset that's helped me not only to find opportunities, but also to keep possession of them and help those around me win.

# BREAKING OUT!

Every action is derived from a thought. Your thoughts are derived from your mindset. If your beliefs empower you and you are determined to unlock your potential, there are very few limits to how far you can go.

★ **Imagine the possibilities**
What big dream or idea would you chase down if NOTHING was in your way?

★ **Believe in yourself**
Do you believe that you are capable of greatness? If not, what is stopping you?

★ **Get a strength coach**
Who is your strength coach? If you don't have one yet, consider people who can challenge you and push you to be better.

★ **Have determination**
What are you determined to do? If you don't have a mission yet, are you determined to find it?

★     ★     ★

∽ There is strength in your potential ∾

# ❧ BEDTIME STORY ❧

*End of Day 1 - 10:37 pm*
*Wow! It has been an unbelievable day. It's really unique that Chandler and I are together again in the house we were raised in without adult supervision. This place is so full of memories and funny stories. I found a box of pictures under Mom and Dad's bed this evening. Chandler is giving me a hard time for how many years I decided to stick with the bowl cut, and I'm giving Chandler a pretty good ribbing for smiling in his sports portraits like a Girl Scout who just sold 20 boxes of cookies. Softy.*

*I can already tell that writing this book is going to teach me a lot and challenge me artistically in a completely new way. This will be the longest song I've ever written! I'm glad Chandler is here coaching me and pushing me along. He might as well have a whistle in his mouth. He keeps saying things like "Don't eat that. It will take too long to prepare and we'll get off schedule." But we haven't started punching each other in the face yet, so today was a big win.*

# NIGHTCAP

## DAY 1: YOUR MINDSET

★ Fitting in is overrated ★

★ Be willing to break the rules ★

★ Challenge normal ★

★ You can replace your limiting beliefs ★
with empowering beliefs

★ Your past does not determine your future ★

★ The good that you're capable of is worth the work ★

★ You're going to need help - and there are people who will help you ★

★ We all need a strength coach. Find yours ★

★ Determination is more valuable than talent ★

★ Empowering beliefs and determination will unlock your potential ★

★ Your mindset will determine your success ★

*p.s. This is the earliest I've gone to bed in eight years! Coincidentally, the last time that happened was on this exact mattress. Home.*

# DAY 2
## YOUR ACTION

# UNLOCKING YOUR PURPOSE

... and your confidence

CHANDLER FOUND THIS BIG BOW IN MOM'S CHRISTMAS STUFF ... AND PUT IT ON MY HEAD ....

*12/22/12 - 9:00 am*

*Mornin'. We're still in Walhalla, SC, at our parents' house. Coffee's on. Feeling good. Oh, yeah before I forget — It's my birthday‼ And what better way to celebrate than to start another mind mapping exercise & outline. (I wish there were a font for sarcasm.) For the record, this is the first time I've ever done an outline in my life. In high school, I would write the paper and then go back and do the outline. I now realize that's exactly why it took me 7 hours to write a three page essay. 10 minutes on the clock, and ... go.*

 *"Show Me How To Live" by Audioslave*

# THE PURPOSE OF WORK

I stumbled upon something fascinating last week. I'm not sure what led me to look it up, but I started reading about the Garden of Eden in the Bible. It was interesting to me that the first mention of man's purpose was simple: to work and maintain the garden. I grew up in church so I'm familiar with the Genesis account of creation, but it seems to me that churches put their own spin on the Garden of Eden ... follow me here:

In Sunday school I learned that the Garden of Eden was paradise created for Adam and Eve's pleasure. It was implied that they had a life of leisure until they rebelled against God. As punishment, the party was over and they were forced to work and settle into life as we now know it.

Now let's look at what the book actually says about humans and why we were created:

"The Lord God took the man, and put him into the Garden of Eden to work it and take care of it." Genesis 2:15, The Bible, KJV

Man's first purpose, according to the Bible, was to work in the Garden of Eden, taking care of God's creation. Adam was a gardener! And this is before he and Eve rebelled against God. Man was created to work! This may not strike you as exciting, but to me it answers the age-old questions, "What is the purpose of life?" and "What is my purpose?" Work isn't God's way of *punishing* man. Work is God's way of purposing man. It just makes sense. Meaningful work strengthens our bodies, sharpens our minds, develops our communication, births creativity, and brings great satisfaction when the task at hand is completed.

It's not just a job; it's your purpose. It's not just a talent; it's a garden. Work it!

# A DEEP WELL OF CONFIDENCE

You've probably been told to be confident or act confidently, as if the boldness to pitch your idea or the courage it takes to put your art on display is a simple on/off switch in your brain. It's not that simple.

Where does confidence come from? And can you get more if you want more? I believe the seed of confidence really does originate in your mind.

**The seed of confidence can be planted in the mind ... but it will only take root in the heart if it's watered by hard working hands.**

During the Great Depression, kids had no choice but to work. Everyone pitched in because hard work put food on the table and a roof over their heads. What it also gave them was a lifelong, quiet, selfless self-confidence that made them the STRONGEST generation of Americans. Hard work is full of lessons you can't learn anywhere else. Every new job you complete is a mini success and before you know it, you have a wealth of both skills and confidence.

My parents were in a better financial situation during Chandler's first ten years than they were in my first ten years. Many of the chores that I had to do growing up, like cutting firewood, working the garden, and helping mom sell clothes at our yard sales were no longer necessary by the time Chandler came along. However, although Mom and Dad could have spared my brother the hard work to give him "a better life," as the ideology goes, my parents' philosophy is that work and challenges create opportunities for what Dad calls "many mini successes." By the time we both left home there was very little we couldn't build, grow, mow, or repair.

**HARD WORK + MANY MINI SUCCESSES = CONFIDENCE!**

It doesn't take half a lifetime to develop confidence. New challenges are the key. It's easy to get into a rut or a comfortable routine that prevents you from challenging yourself. Break out! Find a group of people that do something you find challenging and interesting. It can be physically demanding like skateboarding, rock climbing, or yoga. Or mentally demanding like video game design or learning to play music. The risk is worth the rewards and you'll probably meet a few new friends in the process.

---

"I play to win, whether during practice or a real game. And I will not let anything get in the way of me and my competitive enthusiasm to win."
— Michael Jordan

---

# "TO DO GOOD IS EXPECTED."

"This is bull crap," I thought to myself, but I didn't dare say it to my dad. I had just brought home my first all-A's report card. When I triumphantly presented it to him, I expected a big pat on the back, words of affirmation, maybe some stroking of my ego, and a photocopy on the fridge. Ultimately, my plan was to hit him up for a raise on my allowance or, better yet, to establish a CA$H for GRADES program like my buddy Ben Watkins worked out with his parents. Much to my surprise, I was totally denied. Dad signed the report card and handed it back to me without a word.

**⁊⁊**  Jr. Me: "Did you *look* at it?" I asked as he was reading the newspaper.

Dad: "Yes."

Jr. Me: "I GOT ALL A's!"

Dad: "I see that."

Jr. Me: "Yeaaaaah. So I was thinking. Ben's dad gives him money for making good grades. $10 for an A, $5 for a B, $1 for a C."

Dad: "How many A's did he get?"

Jr. Me: "Only one. I know if I made all A's that would be a lot of money, so I'm okay with making $5 for an A, $3 for a B, and you don't have to pay me for a C."

At the time I thought this spirit of compromise made my plea bulletproof, and this deal — which GUARANTEED my parents good report cards — a BARGAIN!

My dad's counter-offer sucked.

**⁊⁊**  Dad: "How about $0 for an A?"

Jr. Me: "What??! But I did GOOD!"

Dad: "To do good is expected."

He went on to explain that money shouldn't affect whether I choose to live up to my potential or not. With the proper amount of studying and effort, I was capable of making good grades, therefore he expected me to make good grades. This high standard of excellence was then applied to everything I decided to do — pitching in Little League, piano lessons, starting a recording studio business in high school, forming my first rock band, Knights of Dei (*which beat NEEDTOBREATHE in B93.3's Battle of the Bands — I'm just saying*). What was expected of me became what I expected of myself.

### Stop competing with the competition.
### Start competing with *yourself*.

Call it boredom. Call it "making the goal fun." Call it whatever you want. It works. When you start thinking in terms of competing against yourself, powerful wheels of growth start to turn. You're no longer satisfied with first place, nor are you defeated by loss. If I finished second place in a race but set a new personal best; THAT was a victory. If I won third place at a talent show, but had previously been too afraid to even try; THAT was a victory.

When you compete with yourself, you can consistently raise the bar for your performance and your personal best will often exceed the competition. Why??? Unlike people who are content with being slightly better than the guy in second place, you are competing in an entirely different race. You're trying to break your old record. You are raising the bar for yourself. After all, second place in your small town is probably not that fast. You can't get lazy if you want to compete on a larger playing field.

When you compete with yourself, there's nowhere to go but up. Don't let someone else set the bar for you.

# BREAKING OUT!

In what specific area of your life would you like to gain more confidence?

★ What is one mini-success you can shoot for this week to begin to build that confidence?

★ What is one specific challenge you're ready to take on this week to compete against your personal best?

Start TODAY!

★     ★     ★

∽ There is strength in your purpose ∽

# CHAPTER 5

# DO IT NOW

Winning head-to-hand combat with procrastination,
perfectionism, and paralysis by analysis

*Look what I found on our break! A sign I made when I was little.*

*12/22/12- 2:02 pm*
*This reminds me of having to dig potatoes and pick green beans when I was about 10. I tried to make a deal with Mama that I wouldn't eat any vegetables for a whole year if it meant that I didn't have to help get them in from the garden. No such luck.*

*So after failed petitions to compensate me for my hard work in the garden, I finally asked my dad, "Why are we out here working all day when Mom is just gonna give half of the produce away?! Can you at least let me try to sell some of the extra?!" He did, but alas, my first business wasn't a success. I probably should have put a little more time into the marquee.*

 *"When a Heart Breaks" by Ben Rector*

"I never worry about action, but only about inaction."
- Winston Churchill

# HOW TO BEAT THE P.E. #1s

In law enforcement, P.E. #1 is code for Public Enemy #1. It identifies the number one threat to the public.

If you are someone who creates, then you know, with great pain, the enemy inside you that holds you back. It takes on 3 common forms. These private enemies are Progress Eliminators.

★ Procrastination.
★ Perfectionism.
★ Paralysis by Analysis.

*The goal is to get your ideas past these hurdles and to the finish line.*

# HOW TO BEAT PROCRASTINATION

This book never would have happened if it weren't for my brother. The idea of writing a book terrified me. While I have a few of the ingredients needed — a message that I'm passionate about, credibility with my tribe, and a deep desire to help others — I was battling some pretty intense internal resistance. *"What if people hate what I create?"* *"I'm not an author."* *"Some of my best friends are established authors ... they don't pretend to be musicians!"*

**"**    Chandler: "Do you believe in this or not?"

Seth: "I do! It's just that ... I don't have TIME!"
(That was the excuse I gave him. Heard that one before?)

C: "We're gonna write this book in one week over Christmas break."

S: "Oh, really?" (Translation: "You've lost your mind!")

C: "Or we can overthink this and procrastinate so it never gets done."

S: "Yeah ...." (Dadgummit ... He's right.)

C: "We've gotta 'Do It Now.'"

At that point, it clicked with me because I knew exactly what he was referring to. My brother used to be a big procrastinator and one day our loving mother decided to teach him a lesson. She wrote "Do it now" on sticky notes and put them on every piece of unfinished business he had lying around the house.

Unfinished homework – Do it now.

His clothes that *she* had folded that *he* was putting off taking to his room – Do it now.

Unwashed dishes – Do it now.

His Barbie dolls and everything else he always left on the kitchen counter

# Do it now

Mom has always been committed to doing certain things right away so that she doesn't have to deal with the fallout later. She folds newly dried laundry right away so it doesn't wrinkle, she gathers and preserves the harvest so that it doesn't spoil in the garden. One of her great strengths is her efficiency. No time or energy is ever wasted.

Putting something off creates more work. If you wait, you have to remember to do it later or write it on a to do list, then, as you keep putting it off, you read it on that to do list over and over. By the time you muster up the willpower to execute the task, you feel zero inspiration or excitement for it. You know the drill.

"Do it now" is an easy way of preventing that.

"Do it now" empowered Chandler. It clicked. He hated his bad habit of putting things off. Before "Do it now," he was outgunned in the fight against procrastination. Today, he's the most productive person I know and he uses his own version of Mom's "Do it now" sticky notes. I use them all the time AND THEY WORK!!

Before I go to sleep each night, I put these on work and life related items that need to be my top priority for the next day. They prevent me from getting distracted and help me focus the day's energy on what really counts. I'm able to give the time savings to people and things that really matter. Make your own version and try them!

# HOW TO BEAT PERFECTIONISM

Perfectionism = overthinking it.

My name is Seth Bolt, and I'm a perfectionist.

Some would say it's easier to quit drinking than to silence perfectionism. Maybe they should have Perfectionists Anonymous meetings. Wait, I've already told you my full name. Never mind.

Oh, how I wish I could have the time back that I WASTED on little projects that, at the time, *had* to be completed and *had* to be perfect.

Yes, I know you want the thing to be great. Every good artist does. But, like my Aunt Lynne says, "*Is the juice worth the squeeze?*" Not every project is worth all of your time.

As a recovering perfectionist, I do battle with this artistic disease every day. My brother, also a recovering perfectionist, has come up with a way to beat that as well. It's a method he calls "On the clock."

PUT YOURSELF ON THE CLOCK,

NOT UNDERNEATH IT.

"On the clock" works by assigning time limits to tasks. By assigning a very defined amount of time to a project, you eliminate the possibility of losing track of time. This has been especially helpful to me the past two days. I would still be writing and erasing chapter 1 or checking twitter or instagram (@DrSethBolt — follow me!) if it weren't for the timer I can see out of the corner of my eye. I feel pressure to finish on time, so I'm not allowing myself to get hung up on the details. The time constraints Chandler has put on writing each chapter have prevented me from browsing the Internet for fact checking or the exact wording of a quotation, which means saving time on clicking other links or seeing something that triggers a thought that leads me on a rabbit trail to details land. Of course there will be details I'll need to check later, and probably revisions to make, but right now the goal is to complete a draft manuscript in one week.

Try giving yourself a very defined amount of time to complete a task, meet your deadline, and move on.  Short projects become long projects when they aren't given short deadlines. Get into the habit of forcing yourself to live by the clock.  This way, projects don't take all your time ... they take only as much time as you have decided in advance to give them. Putting yourself on the clock is a very potent way of working.

The pace of our productivity is directly linked to the amount of time we think we have to complete a project. If a project only requires 30 minutes, but we have an hour to do it in, we'll find a way to fill the time. For example, I recently gave an intern at my recording studio an assignment. "Repaint this little room today." It dawned on me a few minutes later that "today" was a vague time frame and the job should only take until lunchtime, but I kept quiet to see what would happen.

Sure enough, by 11am, 80% of the work was complete, but the job ended up taking all day because he found some little trouble spots to pick at and obsess over, even though they were out of sight and unlikely to ever be noticed. The next day we noticed that the final 20% he painted towards the end of the day didn't match the 80% he painted that morning. He got lost in the details. I wasn't mad because I'm often guilty of doing the same thing. I should have asked him to finish by lunchtime and given him the afternoon off. He could have done touchups and cleanup the next morning for thirty minutes instead of spending another half day trying to get rid of a line in the middle of the wall.

When you put time limits on projects and stick to them, you'll find that you play more, exercise more, give more time to loved ones — you know, all the things that CLEAR YOUR HEAD — and you can schedule time (in advance) to revisit your work … instead of letting projects linger on because you're getting lost in the details.

# HOW TO BEAT
# PARALYSISBY ANALYSIS

Paralysis by analysis = paralyzed by possibility.

Paralysis by analysis is a combination of procrastination and perfectionism. Do you know people who put off making a decision because they want to make the perfect decision? They probably spend way more time on research than development. Their perfectionism causes them to spend all of their energy on investigating every little detail. And after a while they are either too tired to make the perfect decision or they are paralyzed by all of the possibilities, so they procrastinate and delay making a decision altogether. They have seven shopping tabs open in their Internet browser — but didn't make a purchase. They can't go out to eat without first Yelping every restaurant in town. And once they get there, they have to send the waiter away several times because they "need a little more time to think." And by "them" I mean "me." My dad's the same way. One year he was in charge of booking the family vacation and we didn't go anywhere. His excuse was that there were TOO MANY places to go and not enough time to check them all out. This was a heated conversation that took place two weeks prior to the scheduled "vacation":

❛❛ Seth: "So we're going nowhere?!"

Dad: "We can go somewhere if we can book a place, but the book they gave us from the timeshare place is 2" thick and I'm not going to have time to finish reading it."

Mom: "You're reading about every listing in the directory?!"

Dad: "How else are we gonna know what our options are!? I didn't even know where to start looking!"

Chandler: "You just pick something — like the beach, or the mountains — it doesn't really matter as long as you pick something! You picked nothing. You just read the directory. That doesn't book a vacation!"

# MOTIVATION

One of the biggest contributing factors to keeping yourself moving and getting things done is motivation. Motivation is a combination of focus, inspiration, rewards, and even physical health. Motivation is a choice, and choosing to be motivated is something you have to do on a daily basis — maybe even several times throughout the day. Here are some tricks I use to motivate myself:

## Stay focused

★ 5 minutes of journaling each morning about the most important goals for the day — and how they feed into your long-term dreams.

★ Make the first hour of your day highly productive by being PROactive and not REactive. Tackle the highest priorities for the day before checking social media/text/email or watching the news. One uninterrupted hour of proactive work will give you confidence and momentum and dramatically decrease stress.

## Seek inspiration

★ 10 minutes of reading an author who inspires you or listening to an audio-book while getting ready or during the commute to school/work.

★ Join (or start) a group of people with similar goals who want to serve as motivators and mentors to each other. Chandler and some of his friends use an app called "Lift" that reminds them to do 100 pushups a day. They can see each other's progress and hold themselves accountable. The daily goal can be anything you want it to be and it's an excellent facilitator of encouragement.

## Reward yourself

★ Give yourself small rewards at the end of small accomplishments — maybe 15 minutes of loud music (hopefully NEEDTOBREATHE!), a coffee break, or a social media check-in.

★ Give yourself bigger rewards at the end of bigger accomplishments — maybe a weekend evening out after a week of solid work that moved you closer to your goals.

★ Set a specific reward tied to a specific achievement: If I can complete this tough project well — I'm taking next weekend off.

## Be healthy

★ Physical activity can help shake off sluggishness and lack of focus. When my band is in the recording studio, disagreements and arguments are stressful and sometimes bring the creative process to a halt. That's why taking a break and tossing a football around is like a giant reset button.

★ Stress makes good decision-making even harder. When you feel like you're about to hit a wall (or your boss or best friend in the face), call a time out for a mandatory Frisbee toss. Restarting with a clear head will actually save time. Finally, if you have an hour and really want to feel like a new person, try hot yoga. Tons of health benefits and NO running!!

★ Rest. Other people keep themselves focused and working hard with the promise of a 20-minute nap in the afternoon. This is another nice "restart" and can empower the second half of your day. I usually take a nap a few hours before a show.

# BREAKING OUT!

## DO IT NOW!

This week, before you end your work-day and before you go to sleep at home, put "Do it now" sticky notes on the things that are your top priorities for work and life tomorrow. Then do them first, before anything else.

★ What are some ways, specific to your personality, that you can keep yourself motivated this week?

★       ★       ★

∾ There is strength in your action ∾

# SIMPLICITY

The $624 billion dollar secret

**12/22/12 - 4:00 pm**
*Used our ten minute break to toss around a football that my brother gave me for my birthday! Still on schedule. Might grab a bite to eat after chapter six. Wish Mom was here to cook one of her amazing Southern specialties, but they're on vacation and we have the house to ourselves. Maybe I can talk Chandler into eating at Puerto Nuevo, my favorite Mexican restaurant, so I can get El Burro de la Roqueta. Mmm - wait, what am I saying? It's my birthday. We're going to Puerto.*

 *"Live Forever" by Drew Holcomb and The Neighbors*

You have to respect a guy who whittled down RELATIVITY to $E=MC^2$.
There aren't many people who can explain the universe in 5 symbols.

---

"If you can't explain something simply, you don't
understand it well enough."
- Albert Einstein

---

# O$^{VER}$COMPLICATION

When's the last time you called (insert your phone provider's)
customer support? If you have hair, did you want to pull it out by
the end of the call? For a company whose industry is communication,
you would think that simple problems would have simple solutions!!!
*(DEEP BREATH.)*

Simplicity is getting harder and harder to find, which is why it's
becoming more and more valuable. People are willing to shell out big
bucks for simple.

---

"It has one button, no user manual,
and EVERYONE knows how to use it. - Amazing!"
- Will.I.Am., Black Eyed Peas on the iPad

---

Apple is now the wealthiest company in America, and every
business is studying their methodology. People worship their
products - stand in line to buy them and brag about owning them.
But the company's success didn't happen overnight. Back In 1997,
Apple was 90 days from bankruptcy.  Something was broken. So
they went in a different direction. Instead of making dozens of
mediocre products, they simplified and focused all of their energy
on making a handful of amazing products. Steve Jobs famously axed
70% of the company's hardware and software products in an effort
to simplify their focus.

He walked into the board room and drew a box with four squares that looked like this:

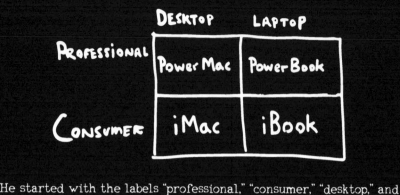

He started with the labels "professional," "consumer," "desktop," and "laptop." Then he said instead of making dozens of computers and gadgets, we're going to make four computers. Anything that doesn't fit into these boxes has to go. This allowed them to apply their energy to "putting the customer before the technology" by creating beautiful computers that were very easy to use. The boxes were filled in with PowerMac, PowerBook, iMac, and iBook. The results were epic, focused, and highly profitable.

------------------------------------------------------------

"Amazingly Simple. Simply Amazing."
- Apple iMac advertisement (1998)

------------------------------------------------------------

At time of writing, Apple's net worth is $624 billion and climbing. Since the iMac they have consistently delivered products that embody their commitment to simplicity.

How can you apply this to your business or to your own life? If you are an entrepreneur, how can you make a product that is superior, not only from a technical or artistic standpoint, but that is also superior in the way that the world interacts with it? On a personal level, how can you simplify the areas of your life that have become overly complicated?

Mastering "simple" requires innovation. The maxim "Life is complicated" could be restated, "Life requires innovation." You can accept complication or challenge it. Simple isn't easy. It requires commitment, but the long-term life enrichment is simply amazing. Take some time to simplify your routines. If you're a person who gets lost in the details, force limits on the number of options you allow yourself.

# Forced limitations force innovation!

My band is in the studio right now making our fifth record for Atlantic Records. We've decided to use "forced limitations force innovation" by limiting the amount of overdubs (where we record additional sounds on an existing recording). This is forcing us to be more creative on our instruments so that we don't rely on an orchestra and a horn section to complete the song. On *The Reckoning*, our last album, some songs had over 160 different parts! That's not a good thing; the human ear can only focus on three sounds at one time. Having way too many parts was the result of having unlimited time, unlimited resources, and no one telling us when to stop. We didn't have a plan that simplified or focused our effort, and as a result, the record-making process got incredibly complicated and stressful. This time we've limited ourselves to 16 tracks. That commitment to simplicity has created opportunities for us to grow as a band. Our recording process is much better because it's more focused.

My cell phone used to be my biggest time waster, so I *forced* time limits on my usage, which forced me to *create* new ways of getting the same job done more quickly. By no means have I mastered simplicity, but I want to share a few of the ideas that work for me.

**1. Use a real alarm clock** – Remember those? They don't have email or social media built into the screen, but they get the job done and get my day off to a fast start.

**2. Un-unlimit your texting** – Would you look at that! I just got a text! But this is my writing time and my mantra is, "Own your phone; don't let it own you!" When I have something important I need to get done, I put my phone on silent and out of sight. When I'm done, or if I need a break, I'll leave that space – go outside if it's nice – and respond accordingly. If something is really important,

I'll call. Likewise, my friends know to call me if they need my immediate attention. I'm not a great multi-tasker. In fact, I do terrible work when my focus is divided. Eliminating the distraction of my cell phone allows me to quiet the chaos.

**3. Limit all screen time** — A phone is probably the most distracting, since it usually goes everywhere with us. But think about all the other "screens" that take up your time — computer, tablet, television. We often get lost in these distractions, losing minutes or hours watching mindless reality TV or playing games. Just like with your phone, give yourself a time limit and stick to it.

**4. Spend your time doing only what you can do** — Recover hours of your time every day by simplifying your routines. Does the task absolutely have to be done? Can someone else help you do it? Can you afford to pay someone to do it? Time is your biggest asset and you need to make sure that you spend it doing those things that only you can do. Automate everything that doesn't require your attention!

**5. Set a Schedule/Make a Plan** — Sometimes we make things more complicated simply by not sticking to a schedule or a plan. We get bogged down by other tasks, forget about important appointments, or end up doing things more than once because we didn't do them right the first time. For example, how many times a week do you have to go to the grocery store? Are you "just running in" a few times a week? If you made a meal plan and went shopping once a week, you'd save lots of time — and money.

Work for simplicity. It will work for you.

# BREAKING OUT!

★ What is one daily task you can simplify, eliminate, or automate?

"Forced limitations force innovation."

Can you think of a project or process that needs simplicity? Maybe it's the way you write papers for school or the way you pick out your clothes in the morning. Force a limitation on that task. Maybe Chandler's "10 minute brainstorm/10 minute outline/90 minutes of writing" will allow you to write 90% of a paper in half the time.

Force a limitation on the number of options you give yourself. A closet full of possibilities can delay the start of your day, not to mention, create an unnecessary mess. Give yourself two options, pick the best one, and move on.

★     ★     ★

❧ There is strength in your simplicity ❧

# BEDTIME STORY

**DRSETHBOLT** ⚙

♥ **749 likes**

**drsethbolt** Feliz Cumpleaaaaños aaaa miiii! - thank you so much for all the birthday wishes! I feel very loved and strangely at home in this Mexican ball cap. Also a big shout out to my compadres at Puerto Nuevo, Hector and Jimmy Lion.

*End of Day 2 - 11:45 pm:*
*We made it to Puerto. Great birthday.*
*Wonderful siesta. Time for bed.*

*p.s. I'm not a real doctor.*

*p.p.s. That started as a joke because when my band started flying to concerts we were advised to sign up for frequent flyer miles programs. Southwest had a little drop down box for Mr., Mrs., and Dr. A few weeks later, I got my degree in the mail.*

*p.p.p.s. No offense, real doctors.*

# NIGHTCAP

## DAY 2: YOUR ACTION

★ Stop competing with the competition ★
Start competing with yourself

★ To do good is expected ★

★ Many Mini Successes - Confidence ★

★ Do it now ★

Avoid the P.E. #1s
★ Procrastination ★
★ Perfectionism ★
★ Paralysis by Analysis ★

★ Put yourself on the clock. Not underneath it ★

★ Make the first hour of your day PROactive, not REactive ★

★ Imagination Time isn't a waste of time; it keeps you from wasting time ★

★ Forced Limitations Force Innovation ★

★ Mastering simplicity requires innovation ★

★ Work for simplicity. It will work for you ★

# DAY 3

## YOUR INFLUENCES

# YOUR INFLUENCES

How your five closest friends are like the Food Pyramid
– and why they can't all be Pop – Tarts™

*12/23/12 – 9:02 am*

*We're driving down to the beach today to meet up with
our folks. We're gonna write one last chapter here and
then another once we get to Edisto Island. Chandler
found his Eagle Scout uniform. Kid's got a lot of badges.
Way more than me. Yes, I'm wearing mine too. He took a
pretty hilarious picture that he'll probably include in his
unique version of Chapter 7.*

*Before this week began, my band recorded demos for
our 5th record. I had the flu for the first week, so I felt
like I was playing catch up the whole time. The book
started immediately after that and I just realized that
I haven't bought Mom and Dad anything for Christmas.
Being an honest brother, I confess this to Chandler, and
being an honest brother, Chandler disapproves with,
"That's embarrassing." Something tells me an unfinished
book doesn't count as a present.*

 *"The Letter" by Joe Cocker*

# YOU SHOW ME YOUR FRIENDS I'LL SHOW YOU YOUR FUTURE

My mom was picky about who I hung out with growing up. She would "get a bad feeling" and intervene. Once she dropped me off at a birthday party and got a bad feeling on the way home. She whipped her car around, let herself into the birthday party and discovered that she didn't like the music coming from the speakers. She complained to the hottest-girl-in-school's mother, then snatched me out of there in front of all my friends all because she heard the word "ass." Needless to say, I wasn't invited to that many birthday parties after that. Little did I know, my graduating class set a school record for alcohol and/or driving related deaths, so maybe Mom's intuition was right after all.

Our parents didn't hover over us. We had lots of freedom. But they made sure our influences were people who would help us grow. Case in point, I first heard the popular phrase "You show me your friends, I'll show you your future" from one of my friends — now that's a good influence. I carried that idiom on to college and surely it is one that I'll pass on to my kids one day.

---

"If you want to fly with the Eagles, you can't continue scratching with the Turkeys."
- Zig Ziglar

---

# AVOID NEGATIVE PEOPLE!

Here are some tips to help fend off negative influences and find positive ones:

**Limit your exposure:** This is simple, but effective. If there is someone in your life who is consistently negative and brings you down, avoid them at all costs. If it's someone you have to interact with, like a co-worker, limit your contact as much as possible — communicate through email, don't accept lunch invitations, whatever it takes.

**Be nice:** Ever heard the phrase, "Kill them with kindness?" It can feel difficult, unfair, and even impossible, but when someone is negative, being nice to them and even finding a positive spin on whatever it is they're complaining about may not change their attitude, but it will help prevent their negativity from affecting your mood and outlook.

**Don't engage:** Sometimes negative people just want an audience. Find a way to politely remove yourself from the conversation.

**Be true to you:** You know what things you love to do and what makes you feel good. Stick to that. Spend time with groups of people with whom you have similar interests. Take a class in something that interests you. You'll likely find like-minded individuals to spend time with who don't drag you down.

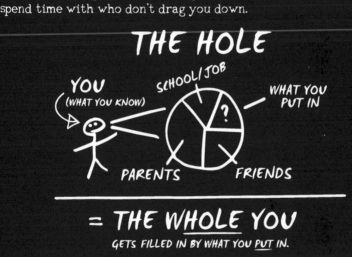

# THE HOLE

YOU (WHAT YOU KNOW)    SCHOOL/JOB    WHAT YOU PUT IN

PARENTS    FRIENDS

# = THE WHOLE YOU

GETS FILLED IN BY WHAT YOU PUT IN.

Since most of what we know we learn from others, it's important to cultivate friendships with a variety of people. You are the average of your five closest friends.

The life that you are designing for yourself is a blend of the blueprints you see around you. Your level of physical activity, how much money you make, the types of parties and events you are invited to, and the quality of advice you're given at the end of an emotional conversation are all determined by the lifestyles of the friends you have in your corner. The person you are on your way to becoming will be heavily influenced by the five people you spend the most time with. Having a well-balanced group of influencers will fill in your missing pieces with whatever goodness you might be missing.

Think of the people in your life or in your past who have helped you grow socially, intellectually, physically, spiritually, and financially. Are they still in your life? If not, have you filled in that missing piece?

Many people allow areas of their lives to suffer because they are looking for everything they need in one best friend. The honest truth is, your friend that keeps your body in shape might not be the same friend to advise you on your new car purchase, but that person will consistently call on you to get outside and take a quick walk with them, so seek them out and keep them in your life.

# ASK THE RIGHT QUESTIONS TO THE RIGHT PEOPLE

One of the most rewarding parts of my job as a musician and as a producer is working with other artists and exchanging new ideas, our predictions regarding the future of the music industry, and more importantly, what inspires us! Most of the time, I'm the one listening, but occasionally, younger, up-and-coming artists will ask me, "What can I be doing better??" What a powerful question!! Think about it. Whether you're asking your boss, your spouse, your coach, your employees, or your customers, it's a question with an answer that almost always inspires positive movement. If nothing more, asking that question shows that you care. Not to mention, it's an easy question to ask your five friends from time to time.

# BREAKING OUT!

Copy down the list below and fill in the names of the friends who improve you in each of these areas. Then put that sticky note on your bathroom mirror or the dash of your car to remind you to spend more time with these people.

**Financially:**_____

**Physically:**_____

**Spiritually:**_____

**Intellectually:**_____

**Socially:** _____

This week, call the two or three people you need most in this period of your life and let them know they play this role for you. ASK FOR INPUT and add value to these people every chance you get.

★     ★     ★

❧ There is strength in your influences ❦

# CHAPTER 8

# YOUR INFLUENCE

## Leave yourself for somebody else

WHEN I PLANTED IT...

... AND NOW!

*12/23/12 - 8:00 pm*
*Made it to the beach. My brother and I listened to*
*"The 4 Hour Work Week" by Tim Ferriss on audiobook in*
*the car. It's awesome and I recommend it to anyone who*
*wants further inspiration for breaking out of mediocrity.*
*Just before we left, Chandler got a great shot of me by*
*this tree — which was just knee-high when I planted it.*

 *"Leave Yourself For Somebody Else" by Phantom Planet*

## "INFLUENCE"

[ˈinflooəns]

*noun* — the capacity to have an effect
on the character, development, or behavior of someone.

Regardless of your age or status, you have the capacity to influence others. And I'll cut right to the chase; the easiest way to increase your influence is by adding value to people. Zig Ziglar said "If you help enough people get what *they* want, you will get what *you* want." Make helping people your mission and you will be very successful. Make helping people your business and you will be richly rewarded.

Perhaps the greatest flaw of capitalism is the underlying assumption that before a business can help others, it must first help itself. Corporations put profit before philanthropy, spend a fortune on advertising to try and connect with consumers, and then give away the scraps for a tax write off. And it often takes decades before they begin to influence, if ever they do. That's a backwards and broken approach. Yet this thinking is so pervasive that consumers — that's you and me — have taken on this same mentality. For example, in a developed nation like the US, it has become "normal" for every member of the household to own a cell phone AND their own car — while our less fortunate global neighbors can't afford shoes or food or medicine or clean drinking water.

Luckily, there is a better way of doing business and living life. Business and helping people should not be two different things. In fact, when entrepreneurs make benevolence part of their purpose for doing business, they tend to influence their customers. And their customers tend to support them because they want to be influences as well.

---

"People don't buy WHAT you do. They buy WHY you do it."
                      - Simon Sinek

---

Consider TOMS Shoes. I guess I've gotten a little more used to them, but I'm still positive they look *way* better on girls than they do on guys. But never mind my preference for boots over feminine looking slippers. I remember when TOMS first came out and all the cool kids and influencers were deciding whether or not to wear them. TOMS, a rookie player in an industry of giants, had a quality product that was unique. Fifty years ago, that was all you needed to be successful. But the world has changed and the ability to produce a quality product that is unique is only half of the equation to becoming successful. The ability to connect is now just as valuable if not more valuable.

Years ago, NEEDTOBREATHE toured with a band called Sanctus Real, and a few of its members had bought TOMS when they first came out. Night after night, fans would ask these guys about their shoes, and the guys would respond: "They're TOMS! It's a cool new shoe company. For each pair of TOMS that you buy, they give away a pair to an impoverished person." I'd imagine that most people's first introduction to TOMS was quite similar.

TOMS shoes was successful because they had a cause that connected. Their mission was more than making money. Their mission was to help people. So instead of advertising what they were selling, they advertised their buy-one-give-one model and why they were selling it. Instead of saying, "This is our unique shoe. This is why it's a superior shoe. You should buy some." They said, "We're on a mission to help people. We believe in using every one of our successes as an opportunity to help someone in need. We also sell shoes. Wanna buy some?" See the difference?

It's not often that a company gives away as much as it sells, and it's rare that consumers get to buy a product and simultaneously do that much good for people in need! The design of the shoe got people's attention long enough to mobilize the company's message. Once people heard the message, they related to the soul of the company.

## WHAT YOU *DO* IS PROOF OF WHAT YOU *BELIEVE*

You don't have to be an entrepreneur or give tangible gifts to increase your influence. Encouragement, love, and appreciation are free to give and priceless to the recipient. Here are a few examples of how you can increase your influence:

**Dream bigger for others than they dream for themselves!**
We all have self-doubt. Encourage others to ignore theirs. Share with them the confidence you have in them! Reaffirm those ideas each time you're with them.

**Be the encouragement those around you need!** A friend of mine uses what he calls an "encouragement rock". It's a smooth stone about the size of a nickel and he keeps it in his pocket. Every time he touches the stone or pulls it out of his pocket, he is reminded to encourage someone.

**Handwrite your "Thank You!"** Texts and phone calls are great; handwritten notes are even better! You can radically impact your friendships, strengthen your network, encourage your mentors and mentees, and dramatically increase your level of influence.

**Become a daily source of value!** How can you serve others? What do you do well that you can share with others?

What insights can you share with people who are just learning what you are already good at? Your influence will grow as people begin to see you as someone who adds value to their life.

# BREAKING OUT!

★ Who are you influencing, or who could you influence?

★ Who is trying to accomplish something that you could support, encourage, or "water" in some other way?

★    ★    ★

∽ There is strength in your influence ∾

# BEDTIME STORY

*End of Day 3 - 11:09 pm*
*There's a picture of me standing by a huge tree at the beginning of*
*this chapter. When I put that tree in the ground it was a knee-*
*high sapling! I watered it and the row of trees in the background*
*every day that summer.*

*Isn't it awesome when something you give and give to becomes*
*something bigger and better than you ever imagined?!*

*I'll never forget showing Ella Mae Bowen this tree when she was 14*
*years old. Ella Mae is a promising artist whose work I have produced*
*and with whom I've co-written. Around the time I showed her this*
*tree, we were doing a lot of "watering" for her music and career*
*as a singer and songwriter. It was hard for her to believe that*
*something that had been planted so small had, in not too much time,*
*became something of such great size.*

*In some ways, it's a parallel to what's happened with my band.*
*When we get stories from around the world about how one of*
*our songs has reached and blessed someone, I'm blown away.*
*NEEDTOBREATHE, the local band that used to rehearse in my dad's*
*garage a hundred feet from this tree, has grown to where we are*
*today not only because of all the "watering" we band-members did,*
*but also because of the help and support we got from our influencers*
*and our amazing fans along the way.*

# ～ NIGHTCAP ～

## DAY 3: YOUR INFLUENCE

★ You show me your friends. I'll show you your future ★

★ You are the average of your 5 closest friends ★

★ The wHOLE you gets filled in by what you put in ★

★ Ask for input ★

★ People don't buy what you do. They buy why you do it ★

★ What you do is proof of what you believe ★

★ Become a daily source of value ★

# DAY 4

## YOUR MOMENTUM

# MANY MINI SUCCESSES

Kick-starting your confidence and your momentum

*12/24/12 - 9:04 am*
*It's Christmas Eve! Mom is cooking breakfast while we write, and Dad is looking at old car magazines and doing his best not to disturb anyone. Mom is very curious about what we're going to say about her. I assure her that 75% of the time it's 100% positive, and I smile. She rolls her eyes and reminds me that she knows where I live.*

*P.S. Had to share a twin bed with my brother last night. It still amazes me that he can't stay on his side of the bed! I can't tell you how many times I woke up to his knee, elbow, or entire back. Zero sleep etiquette. On a positive note, he's finally stopped peeing in the bed. I'm laughing as I type this and now his eyes are full of suspicion. Luckily we're sitting across from one another and he can't look at my writing until we get the book back from the printer. Chandler, wherever you are when you read this, I love you and I'm sorry I'm not sorry! :)*

 *"Just Breathe" by Pearl Jam*

"It's not about what it IS, it's about what it can BECOME."
- Movie trailer for LORAX

# THE BLUEPRINT

My dad never really discussed with me why he made me do certain chores or projects with him. Looking back, he could have made promises about how much I would thank him later or how the lessons I learned while doing a bunch of STUPID, seemingly pointless work were going to prepare me for a successful career. Instead, he just woke me up early every Saturday morning with a moderately convincing Donald Duck voice, "Allll riiiight buddy, it's tiiiime for work." Which kind of implied that fixing the lawnmower or stacking firewood was as fun as Saturday morning cartoons. He wasn't fooling me!

Little did I know, the vast array of building projects we attempted together were giving me chances to build my confidence, build my momentum, and build my future; and in fairness to Mom and Dad, the time together was beautifully orchestrated and vividly animated.

Though my memories of my childhood are colorful, our situation wasn't all that unique. Like many parents raising their first child, Mom and Dad didn't know exactly how their parenting would affect me. They saw work to be done and they needed help doing it. Maybe they thought that making me work on Saturdays would help me learn discipline and would make me stronger, but they had no idea it would develop self-confidence and kick start my momentum!

My parents were determined to get ahead and determined to give me a head start on tackling life. They just barely had life by the horns themselves, but together we managed to stay on for 8 seconds, time and time again. This chapter is about some of those 8-second rides.

*Mechanical bull: My Papa Bolt was a logger. I loved riding the tractor and did it often. At a very young age it was fascinating to me to watch him literally change the world around us.*

# BUILDING A HOME

It was my parents' dream to buy land and build a home that was big enough to raise Chandler and me. They couldn't afford much so the piece of land they bought was in shambles. Before we could begin building our house we had to remove the remnants of a house that had burned to the ground seventy years prior. To make things worse, the land was covered in Kudzu, a Japanese vine that grows a foot per day during the Carolina summers and is nearly impossible to kill. There was no grass, the ground was uneven, with no clear spot for a house, no road, "no nothing." We had to employ every blue-collar trade and skillset imaginable to whip the land into shape and eventually build the house that I would grow up in. Dad didn't know what trade Chandler and I might gravitate to for an occupation, so he taught us as many as he could. Every Saturday was a new adventure in building (Dad's trade), logging (our papa's), farming (something a few of us still do out in the country), auto-mechanics, and lots of troubleshooting.

And every Saturday, my dad made a list of all of the tasks we needed to get done that day. Always, the list seemed too long, and inevitably, before lunchtime, something would break and we'd be put behind schedule. We'd have to work extra hard to get the jobs done or we'd end up working past dinner and I would miss Walker, Texas Ranger. And as we all know, nothing is more motivating than Chuck Norris!

*All the building ... built me.*

Slowly, but surely, we cleared the debris of the burnt down abandoned house and planted a garden. We killed all of the Kudzu. We cut down trees, removed the stumps, leveled the ground, and built a house.

Dad decided it would be cheaper to heat our house and our water with an outdoor wood stove. You have to fill it with a wheelbarrow full of wood per day, so you can imagine how much wood that requires. Mom and Dad both had the APB out for firewood and anytime we'd get a call from someone wanting to get rid of a few trees we'd go through the following process: Saw the trees down. Drag 'em out of the woods. Cut them into smaller chunks. Split the smaller chunks into pieces. Load them in a trailer. Dump the trailer. Stack the wood. (*I hope you can hear the tone of voice I'm using to write this.*) It was hard work, but each trip was an opportunity for many mini successes.

My least favorite chore in the history of least favorite chores was picking up rocks. When it came time to clear the remains of the burnt down house, "Seth, go pick up rocks." When it came time to plant a garden, "Seth, go pick up rocks." When it came time to plant grass, "Seth, go pick up rocks."

**❞❞** Sore-handed me (age 14): "I think I got 'em all."

Dad: "Nope. I still see some. Go pick 'em up."

Jealous me: "Why doesn't Chandler have to pick up rocks? All he ever does is sit on the couch watching cartoons!"
Chandler (age 4): "Mom says my hands are too widdle and I should pwabwy stay inside."

Annoyed me: "Well there's plenty of 'widdle' rocks you can help me with."

Dad: "Chandler, go help Seth pick up rocks."

Chandler: "Now I'm gonna miss the rest of Sponge Bob Square Pants!! SEFF!"

Reinvigorated me: "Yessss!"

Still, there were a hundred and eighty-seven things I would rather have been doing with my brain and my energy than picking up rocks! It was a waste of time and I knew it. I cried. I spit. I resisted. An acre of rocks?! It's impossible. I can't do it. I'll never finish. It's too hard. It's mind numbing. It's hot. On one particularly hot South Carolina Saturday I cursed every stone I touched. It wasn't uncommon for the rickety wheelbarrow to tip over, forcing me to start over. Talk about a test of endurance!

Dad reasoned that it would make me strong. Fourteen-year-old me thought he meant my arms and back. Twenty-nine year old me realizes he was raising the threshold for my mental toughness and preparing me for the discipline, the confidence, and ultimately the momentum it would take to successfully launch PLANTATION STUDIOS, NEEDTOBREATHE, and all the other projects I've been blessed to be a part of.

It would be years before I realized that the building projects, backpacking, chopping wood, and picking up stones, TOGETHER all built my confidence and kick started my momentum. Completing each of these tasks, no matter how small and insignificant they seemed at the time, gave me a sense of accomplishment and helped me understand the idea of being able to do whatever it is that I set my mind to. There is power in small victories. Many mini successes create confidence and unstoppable momentum.

Here are a few of the momentum building "lessons" that work taught me:

★ Consistent effort delivers consistent results. You achieve way more by consistently chipping away at something … instead of having huge spurts of effort followed by equally long lags.

★ The amount of time you spend dreading and complaining about work is directly proportionate to how much longer you will have to work before you're done.

★ You can almost always go a little farther than you think.

★ One way to get really good at something is by starting out not good … and then doing it a bunch of times.

★ Some tasks are one-man-jobs; others get done so much better and faster with help. It's really important to know which is which.

# BREAKING OUT!

Learning a new skill is a mini success and an easy way to boost your confidence and your momentum! Challenge yourself this week. Learn how to do something you've always wanted to be able to do!

 Sew on a button

 Learn to build a campfire (without flammable liquids!)

 Learn how to cook a favorite dish

 Change a tire

 Start a small garden

 Take an elder to lunch and listen

 Make a simple home repair

 Learn to ski (or water-ski)

 Pick up rocks until you cry. Do it for another two hours

★    ★    ★

∽ There is strength in your mini successes ∾

# CHAPTER 10

# READY.
# READY FOR ANYTHING

NEEDTOBREATHE's childhood motto and the secret for maintaining momentum

---

*12/24/12 - 11:05 am*
*I hear the waves crashing the beach every time Mom or Dad opens the door to the little wooden back porch here at the beach house on Edisto Island, and I kinda wish I was sleeping on the beach right now. It occurred to me while writing the last chapter that since I left for a tour in Europe a month ago, I haven't taken a day off. This week is technically my "week off," but I'm glad I didn't wuss out on the pact I made with Chandler. Mom and Dad are reading and probably trying to relax despite our noisy typing. Christmas-eve breakfast is cold now. Sorry, Mom. We slam some homemade muffins during a 5 minute break, hug Mom, walk outside, take a few deep breaths, and we're right back at it. There's no stopping now.*

 *"You Only Live Once" by The Strokes*

---

## THREE ROYAL RANGERS

When I met my band mates Bo and Bear, I was seven and they were eight and nine, respectively. We went to the same church — their dad was the preacher — and on Wednesday nights there was a program for the boys our age called Royal Rangers. It was basically Boy Scouts with some Biblical principles tied into the knot-making. Occasionally we would march around like soldiers because one of the head Rangers was a former Drill Sergeant (that part was freakin' cool). We would start each meeting by saying the Royal Ranger Motto. Like any kind of recitation, everyone used their droniest (that's a word, where I come from) voice mixed with a little tough guy, "I'm in the Army" prepubescent authority.

There aren't many things I can recite from memory that I learned at age 7, but The Royal Ranger Motto is definitely one of them.

In fact, all three of us still know it by heart, and it's one of the first "lyrics" we ever learned together. Every once in a blue moon, we'll be backstage or on the tour bus with a group of people and someone will say, "Ready!" And Bear, Bo, and I will bust into it. Our friends will give us that "What on earth?" look and then crack up. Great party trick. And an even better momentum-building mantra.

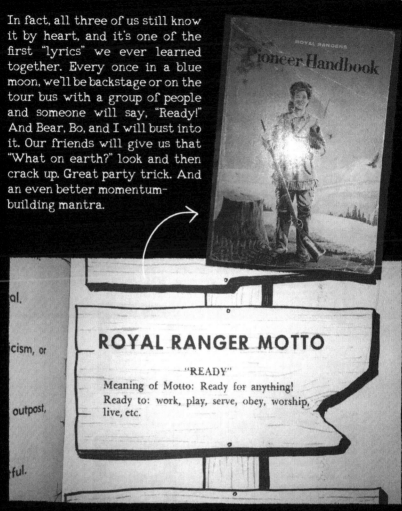

**ROYAL RANGER MOTTO**

"READY"

Meaning of Motto: Ready for anything!
Ready to: work, play, serve, obey, worship, live, etc.

al.

cism, or

outpost,

ful.

---

"Ready. Ready for anything.
Ready to work, play, serve, obey, worship, live, etc."
- The Royal Ranger Motto

---

I'd like to quickly break it down line by line and share how each motif has helped me and NEEDTOBREATHE to succeed. I hope you can draw inspiration from the motto and use it to help you reach your own goals.

## "READY."
[ˈredē]
1 [predicate adjective] fully prepared

Ready is not a verb. You cannot ready. Ready REQUIRES a verb, or an action. You can GET ready (which we talked about on Day 2) and you can STAY ready (which we are going to talk about right now). Both GETTING ready and STAYING ready are actions, and both are equally important.

Just because you do the necessary dieting and exercise to GET into shape doesn't mean you will STAY in shape without continued effort. After working nearly every day from the Spring of 2001 to the Spring of 2006 to get a record deal, NEEDTOBREATHE signed with Atlantic Records — five years of dreaming, practicing, brainstorming, and touring had paid off. (And by paid off I mean, I got a check for $13,000 that was supposed to last me a year. Ha!) Still, it was tempting to sit in front of the proverbial mirror and idly admire our accomplishment. We have a record deal. We can put our faith in the record label now to keep this momentum going for us, right? Wrong.

Back at our hotel room in New York City, before the ink had time to dry on the 200-page contract, Bear launched into his "We haven't made it" speech. It was prophetic truth. Eight years after signing, we still put our boots on every day.

*My expectations of how much the label would help us couldn't have been more flawed.*

No one will ever care about your band or your project as much as you do. Don't slow down. Art, or whatever you are passionate about, might seem like work at times, but count your blessings, stay ready, and march on. Continued effort will keep you ready for the obstacles and opportunities that come your way so that you can maintain your momentum and accelerate to move your project towards the finish line.

## "Ready for anything."

In the context of the Royal Rangers, I always took "Ready for anything." as being prepared to defend. Ready for anything that came at me. Ready for the obstacles and the unexpected. Ready to overcome anything that might slow me down. Maintaining your momentum is essential to reaching your goal, and every day you'll face stumbling blocks that will threaten to slow your progress or trip you up. The night before we were supposed to fly to Atlanta to begin recording our album The Heat, Atlantic called off the session. Even though we had sent in 18 demos in total, the recordings got lost in a pile on someone's desk.

The head of the label had heard only two songs and thought we weren't ready to make an album. The setback would have threatened our small window of recording time and delayed our next tour had we not already secretly begun recording the songs at my studio. Working ahead provided a timely safety net.

You can't predict your future, but you can protect your future. Setbacks aren't setbacks if you're already ahead. Momentum is everything.

---

"If you wait on something to happen, it's gonna be bad.
If you MAKE something happen – it's gonna be good."
– Greg Brewer – my pee wee football coach

---

Our goal has always been to stay a few steps in front of the label. When they say, "Okay, I guess it's time to make a new record, what are your thoughts", we say "Here it is." Because we secretly started working on it the day after the last one was released. We've always done that and it's allowed us to lead the label instead of follow.

This state of ready became the modus operandi for the band, and although I can't say for sure, I'm willing to bet there were a lot of doors we got to walk through simply because we were consistently ready. I remember times when we would practice for an entire week with the motivation that if we got a call on Saturday from someone needing a last minute opening band, we would be ready. There was no promise of a show. But there was always, at least in our minds, the possibility of a show.

And wouldn't you know it, our first tour of the Midwest, actually our first tour ever, came about when we got a call saying, "The scheduled opener had to cancel. If you can be in Chicago in 72 hours, you can have the whole tour opening for Graham Colton!" It felt very rock and roll. 72 hours later, when our feet hit the stage in Chicago, we were a mix of excited, nervous, and high on adrenaline. Had we been unrehearsed, we could easily have been a train wreck that night. Who knows, if we had not been ready to play a good show, Graham could have called his manager and said, "These guys stink. Send 'em home. I'll finish the tour without an opener." Luckily, that wasn't the case. The show went off without a hitch and Graham asked us to join him on several more tours, each one bigger than the last! Each one came at a critical time and each one accelerated our momentum. I'm eternally grateful to Graham, and also to the guys in my band for being ready and staying ready.

## "Ready to work, play, serve, obey, worship, live, etc."

The meter, or tempo, of the motto really picked up speed on the last line. I wish I could just sing it to you, but I'll try to explain. The recitation started out slow, but then finished rather aggressively. "Ready. (pause) ... Ready for anything. (pause) ... Ready to WORK! PLAY! SERVE! OBEY! WORSHIP! LIVE! ETC! — Perhaps the peculiar ending is what made it hook into our brain. Imagine a great crescendo. We would be nearly shouting by the end. The third and final line was always more aggressive, kinda like we were charging enemy lines with a war cry.

WORK! PLAY! SERVE! OBEY! WORSHIP! LIVE! ETC! The intensity implied action. You don't wait for these things to come to you; you make them happen!

These actions were vital to NEEDTOBREATHE's momentum because they taught us to aggressively seek balance, community, and perspective. What is work without play? What is living without service? No matter how big the band gets, we know our place in the grand scheme of things. I'll admit that sometimes we rewrite it and it goes something like this:

*Ready.*
*Ready for anything.*
*Ready to work, work, work, work, work, work, etc.*

Trust me, those aren't our most productive seasons. Have you been there?

It's tough if you're an artist, isn't it? But there's only so much you can pour out of your cup before you have to LIVE again and refill it. There are a lot of ways that you can be ready in your own life. Here are a few examples:

**Have an emergency fund.** Set aside money every month and don't spend it! Then, when your car needs new tires or your refrigerator goes out, you're not stressed about how you'll pay for the unexpected expense.

**Work ahead.** If you're in school and you have a syllabus for your classes, try to read ahead. Not only will you be prepared and not scrambling to read the night before, but you'll also have some wiggle room if you fall behind in another class.

**Plan for winter.** We all have certain times of the year that are difficult for us — some people hate the holidays, sometimes the anniversary of a sad event in your life can drag you down for days and weeks, or a certain time of year is incredibly stressful at work. Stress and emotional turmoil can drag us down and make us lose momentum very quickly. Take steps so that time of year isn't so difficult for you. Ask family and friends for extra support or plan fun things that make you happy and bring you peace.

**Learn to say no.** Most people want to help whenever they can, whether it be taking on extra projects at work, volunteering, or keeping family commitments. But if you are scheduling too much, you can quickly become burnt out. In order to help others, you also have to take care of yourself. It's okay to say no if taking on extra responsibility causes you too much stress.

**Learn from your mistakes.** As I said in Chapter 2, you can learn from failure. If you make a mistake, be sure to figure out how you could have been better prepared so that it doesn't happen again.

# BREAKING OUT!

Momentum is a precious, precious thing. It's hard to gain and easy to lose. If you can maintain it in the storm, you can accelerate it in the aftermath. Continuous effort keeps you ready, so find ways to grow.

Be Practicing. Be Planning. Be Playing. Be Preparing.
Be Perfecting. Be Poised.

★ What are some ways that you can be ready in your work or personal life? Make a list and then take some actionable steps toward making a plan.

*Stay ready, my friends.*

★          ★          ★

~ There is strength in your momentum ~

# THE DISCIPLINE TO "DO"

## How the will to fight-on will end in a win

> *12/24/12 - 2:33 pm*
> *The cardboard writing map we created a few days ago*
> *has traveled everywhere with us, but the tape is wearing*
> *out and it keeps falling to the ground in a slow, overly*
> *dramatic fashion. It kinda spooks Mom every time and*
> *she runs to keep it from falling. God bless my ardent,*
> *faithful mama.*

 *"Not Alone" by Seabird*

## WHEN A HIT AIN'T A HIT

Most of the time, doing what you love isn't lucrative at first. NEEDTOBREATHE played concerts for seven years without any of us seeing a dime of the money we made. It all went right back into "the band." Conversion vans, sound systems, lights … you name it. If you don't think that was frustrating, trust me, by show #1,020, it's frustrating. Even after signing with Atlantic Records, it would be years before we would see any money from concert tickets go into our pockets. We didn't necessarily expect to be rich overnight, but I'd be lying to you if I told you it hadn't crossed our minds a time or two. Bo and I were *convinced* our first record, *Daylight*, was gonna sell a million copies. We just *knew* it. Bear said "No way." Bo and I were *so* sure of it that we bet him $100 on the golf course one day.

I'm too embarrassed to tell you how many copies we sold, but it wasn't a million. It was demoralizing. Here we were, *signed* to a major label, flat broke, and the floodgates of success seemed to be levied.

Meanwhile, rumors circulated around our town that we were rich and had all bought lake houses. I still lived with my parents! *(And continued to do so for another FIVE years. Now THAT is not cool. I may or may not have started calling my parents my "roommates", so I didn't seem like a 24 year-old loser.)*

Even my "roommates" began starting our conversations with, "So what's gonna happen now? Blah blah blah ... plan B."

It was a critical time for the band. It was a critical time for me, personally. The dream I was so close to catching began slipping away from me. My band mates and I knew that a call from our manager saying "Atlantic Records has decided to drop you from their roster" was likely. We were at a crossroads. Our momentum was under attack. Our determination was being threatened by doubt. Nothing was going the way we planned, so *the discipline* to do something productive each day was also evading us. We were frustrated that all the continuous effort and "staying ready" wasn't panning out or paying off.

# HITTING THE WALL

Sometimes working toward your goal is a piece of cake. Yeah, it's always hard work but sometimes you feel inspired, motivated, and on top of the world, so doing the work is no problem. Other times, working towards your goal is a frustrating and nearly impossible task. If *you're* not feeling inspired, motivated, or on top of the world, then you at least need to be disciplined enough so the hard work still gets done. Your momentum may feel like it slams into a wall from time to time. I know mine does. Here are some words of wisdom I've gathered along the way that encourage me and give me the strength and *discipline to do the next right thing:*

* ✦ Remember, doing what you love is the best job in the world.
* ✦ Being an overnight success isn't the goal.
* ✦ The longer you build it, the longer it lasts.
* ✦ Be true to yourself and true to your cause the whole way through.
* ✦ Do the next right thing. Respect is more valuable than riches.
* ✦ You can't make everybody happy. Take some pressure off yourself.
* ✦ If you're waiting on someone else to get you out of a funk, you're choosing to be in a funk for a while.
* ✦ If you're failing at making yourself happy, try making someone else happy.
* ✦ You had the strength to start this journey. You'll find the strength to finish it.
* ✦ This too shall pass.
* ✦ Resilience is a choice that promises productivity.

## "RESILIENT"

[ ri´zilyənt ]

adjective (of a substance or object) able to recoil or spring back into
shape after bending, stretching, or being compressed.
(of a person or animal) able to withstand or recover quickly from
difficult conditions.

# HITTING THE ROAD ... AGAIN

The low point for NEEDTOBREATHE's momentum came seven years
after we began the journey. For seven years we had been asking our
families to stick with us, keep their faith alive, and give us a little
more time. We were broke and broken. We could have slowed down,
given up, cashed out, or backed out, but we decided to keep on ...

"... runnin' down a dream. That never would come to me."
- Tom Petty

We doubled down and promised each other we wouldn't take an
easier road to success if it meant watering down the music. So we
headlined our own shows for 20 people and grew it one fan at a
time. With each tour, we were taking a chance on ourselves. And

we learned a lot of invaluable lessons that way. There may be times when YOU are the only one willing to take a chance on your idea. That's okay. Ask your friends and people you trust if they think the idea is worth going after. They may not be able to support you in a financial way, but if they think your idea is a good one, that knowledge will increase your confidence and help you to go chase it down.

# HITTING THE BIG TIME

Now, when I am asked, "So what was your big break?" I honestly don't know what to say. Our songs have never been Top 40 hits. I've never been on the cover of Rolling Stone (or even inside for that matter)! Again, I can't tell you how many times we had ZERO traction. No one was calling us from the label to tell us the next step to take. No big name headlining bands wanted to take us out as an opener. Yet, we are now in a place where we are making our fifth major label record (something that is virtually unheard of these days), we can play a show anywhere in the United States to at least a thousand people, and we're headlining music festivals now for forty and fifty thousand! So I usually answer the question regarding said "big break" by joking, "Lots and lots and lots of tiny breaks." We've had a lot of small victories, or "many mini successes," and we are blessed with amazingly loyal fans who are as dedicated to us as we are to them!

# BREAKING OUT!

A great tactic for getting more of what you want is to pretend that you have none of it.

★ What is something (tangible or not) that you want more of in your life? If you had absolutely none of this, how would you begin building it?

_____

> "Every morning, before I put on my suit,
> I look at myself in the mirror as if I'm dead broke.
> Then I go out and make something of myself."
> - Michael Porcaro, Owner and founder of Tides Enterprises

_____

★     ★     ★

⌐ There is strength in your discipline ⌐

# ❧ BEDTIME STORY ❧

**End of Day 4 - 12:37 am**
Today's writing focus on momentum hits home for me because recently when people have asked me "So, how's Chandler doing?" my gut response is, "Man, he's doing great. He's got a lot of momentum right now!" And it's true. He's surrounded himself with people who strengthen him. People want him around because he has a brilliant mind for business and a thoughtful way of appreciating people that encourages those he works with. He sends a handwritten "Thank you" card every day! I'm inspired by his mindset, his actions, and his influence. I'm inspired by his momentum. He travels for pleasure more than I travel for business! And I'm jealous! Basically if you drew up a plan for an awesome life where you worked hard for only a few hours a day, made a lot of money, and then had plenty of time left over to spend with friends and family, that would be the perfect description of Chandler. Proud brother moment.

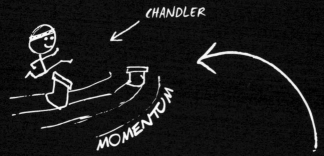

Chandler doesn't like my stick drawings. So naturally, I drew one of him. Kinda looks like he's fist pumping mid-jump.
That part is very true to life.

Every artist and entrepreneur goes through different stages of momentum. Sometimes the swim is easy, sometimes you're treading water, and sometimes you just feel like you're sinking. But if an elephant can sink into the water and rise back to the top, so can you! The dreams placed in your heart weren't put there to tease you. Land may look like it's far away, but keep swimming.

# ⚮ NIGHTCAP ⚮

## DAY 4: YOUR MOMENTUM

★ Many mini successes create confidence and momentum ★

★ Consistent effort delivers consistent results ★

★ You can always go a little farther than you think ★

★ Be Ready ★

★ Getting ready and staying ready are actions ★

★ Working ahead provides a safety net ★

★ Having the strength to fight-on will end in a win ★

★ Do the next right thing ★

★ The longer you build it, the longer it lasts ★

★ Resilience is a choice that promises productivity ★

★ Remember, doing what you love is the best job in the world ★

# DAY 5
# CHRISTMAS DAY

BOWL CUT
VARIATION #36

REAL TEAR

*Christmas Day 1995. Crybaby wouldn't smile.*
*Toy separation anxiety.*

# DAY 6

## YOUR MONEY

# GIVING

The mightiest current of the mighty currency

---

*12/26/12 - 9:12 am*
*Good morning! Final day of writing and we're doing it from a remote cabin in the woods. Seriously! As planned, last night we drove from Edisto Island back to the Smokey Mountains to finish the book in seclusion ... and holy cow, there is NOTHING around here, except for a pond and a large pile of fireworks we bought on the way up here. Buy-one-get-one-free!! I may or may not have spent all my Christmas money in one place. But I need to save my enthusiasm for that adrenaline-filled light show until later tonight because it is currently a very peaceful morning and we don't need anyone responding to a mistaken S.O.S.*

*A MIGHTY CURRENCY*
*This section on money is the one I feel most capable of writing because my parents taught me about giving, debt, and stewardship at an early age. They reinforced these powerful principles often and gave me real life examples of how each were working for or against them. They both grew up poor and had seen money work against their families, and they were determined to turn that around. Having me in their early twenties only added to the challenge.*

*Just before my third birthday, my dad was fired from his job. This happened three weeks before Christmas, so my family didn't exchange gifts that year. Embarrassed and determined never to let the family down again, he started his own company. I watched him build it one brick at a time and I'm proud to say that, unlike 95% of small businesses that fail in the first five years and the 70% of those that fail in the five after that, his business is thriving into its 25th year. I'm also proud to say that my mom and dad have given over half of his income to charity for the last two decades!*

Way to go, Mom and Dad! Thank you for setting that example for me. Many of my peers in the arts community make art because they love it and they try to distance themselves from money so that it doesn't influence their artistic decisions.

That, I applaud, but if you fall into that category, make sure you hire a manager you can trust and then educate yourself enough to double check their work from time to time.

Other artists take a loose approach to their finances for reasons like a lack of financial education or a lack of responsibility. And it's sad, really, because money starts to work against them and it directly limits their flexibility and potential. I've seen close friends blindsided by preventable financial disasters. I've heard numerous stories in green rooms backstage from guys and girls who signed horrible recording and/or publishing contracts simply because they were desperate for the fast cash it would put in their hands. Their lack of a financial education kept them poor, allowed them to be taken advantage of, and cost them a fortune.

So, to my detractors, I make no apologies for putting so much emphasis on money. I'm going to tell you, in a nutshell, the lessons my parents taught me. These lessons handed me the reins to my resources and have filled my life, and the lives of others, with abundant blessings.

A MIGHTY CURRENT
Men born poor have died rich and wealthy people have died destitute. It doesn't matter what you start with, nor does it matter what you end with. All that counts is how you use what you're given. Money is a force to be reckoned with. It's a mighty current that flows in and out of your life daily. Money is either working for you, or it's working against you. Luckily, you can direct the flow of money, if you know how it works!

p.s. If you aren't naturally interested in money, then for the sake of your career and your future family, get interested.

*Just because you're not into money doesn't mean money won't get you into trouble.*

*Ask the people who wake up one day to high credit card debt. Financial misconduct will land you in financial prison. Financial indifference is like a self-ordered stay of execution. Financial education is your ticket to freedom.*

*p.p.s. Today I will be listing a few other resources that perhaps you should consider. The primary lessons and stories in these next few chapters are intended to be broad-brushed strokes that outline the foundation of my financial education and these other resources will color in the important details.*

*I can't overemphasize the value they will add to your life and to the lives of those you will impact. You don't need to have a lot of money to explore these next few topics. These principles work on any scale.*

*While most books on the topic of money focus on its acquisition, I'd like to focus on its offering.*

 *"Supply and Demand" by Amos Lee*

"Almost the unfailing recipe for happiness and success; It is more blessed to give than to receive because in GIVING, although it doesn't seem so, you RECEIVE."
- Archbishop Desmond Tutu

## SAYING "YES" TO GIVING

When I was nine I wanted Nike Air Jordan tennis shoes so badly that I tried every angle of persuasion I could think of with Mom. "You told me to 'be the best I can be', but how am I supposed to be my best if I don't have the best equipment?!" Her laughter mocked my seriousness, so I challenged her charity. "Maybe we could afford a pair if you didn't give our extra money away!"

❞❞  Mom: "Seth! We have extra *because* I give it away!"

    Seth: "Mom, that doesn't make *any* sense."

    Mom: "We are blessed because I bless others."

    Seth: "Well, I wish you would bless *me* with a new pair of shoes."

Instead of *physically* supporting my feet with *temporary* Nikes, my parents *intellectually* supported my life with *lasting* financial education!

And step #1 was a big lesson: Give.

It took me a few years to understand the giving principle that took my parents from dirt poor to debt free. It took no time at all to watch how blessed others were by my mother's generosity!

*Look what I found in the attic! My mom's "Above & Beyond"*
*award for working with underprivileged youth.*
*She was always going above and beyond.*

Before the little room over our garage became NEEDTOBREATHE's first recording studio, it was a temporary shelter for anyone needing a transition to a better life. Since my parents grew up poor, and that's also the way they lived at the beginning of their marriage, one would think that my parents would always choose to make money for themselves if the opportunity presented itself. They could have rented out that space and made money, but they chose to be generous and help those who needed help. And the guest list was a mile long. They hosted a stripper and her 3-year-old daughter, an ex-convict, alcoholics, widows, and the homeless. If someone had genuine need, Mom would sow genuine seed.

# SEED

Mom found a way to explain the concept of giving in a way that I could understand. Like many of the other lessons, she used our garden as an example. "You see this one seed. This will feed our family for weeks, but not unless we plant it." Remember the first time your mind could grasp that abundant amounts of food and life can start with one little seed? Transfer that concept to money!! I know it's hard to plant a perfectly good hundred-dollar bill. Yes, it will take weeks or months for that seed to multiply, so plant often. There are many free ways to bless people, but sometimes absolute needs require money, so here are a few simple ways to plant a blessing in someone else's life.

* Maybe you know a family that could use a grocery delivery.

* If it's winter, consider purchasing coats from a second hand store and giving them to the homeless or underprivileged. This is a great opportunity to involve your children or younger siblings to teach them how easy it is to help others.

* Know a friend who needs a lift? Surprise her with her favorite coffee.

* Make care kits: $10, $20, or $50 can go a long way in the $.99 bins, and make great gifts for friends with upcoming trips or for people in the military.

* Tools: What guy doesn't like tools!? An apron with a few essentials (tape measure, hammer, trim nails, and screwdriver) is a long lasting blessing to a couple that is buying their first home.

"The first five years of running a business
were a struggle because I was only saying "yes" to profit.
When I started saying "yes" to giving, I didn't have to
worry about profit anymore."
– Dad

Around the end of the fifth year of owning his own business, Dad decided not to charge a widow for the necessary repair work she had requested. He paid for the materials and paid his workers their normal wage, but instead of sending her the bill, he sent her a note that said "Amount owed – $0.00. Bless you!" What happened months later was mind blowing! Little did he know, her son-in-law was one of the largest building contractors in the area, and he was so impressed with my dad's generosity and good moral character that he asked him to help build all his new houses! That building contract was worth nearly one hundred times the value of the job he donated to the widow!

Give and you will be blessed. My parents understood that. That's why they taught me the power of giving, first.

# BREAKING OUT!

Here are some ideas for how you can plant your next seed:

★ Give 10% of your income this month to your church or favorite charity.

★ Maybe you know a single mom who would really enjoy getting her nails done and an afternoon of babysitting.

★ Pass it on! Do you have items around your house that you aren't using? If they are new or have a lot of life left, consider giving them to someone who could use them.

★ Leave an extra-large tip for your server.

★ Give your pizza delivery guy a gas card with your tip.

★ Buy a book for a friend if you come across one that they would enjoy. (100% of the profit from this one goes to charity if you want to double your impact! :)

★ Invite someone who lives alone out for dinner.

★ Short on money this week? Sow seeds of encouragement! Give kindness.

★   ★   ★

❀ There is strength in your giving ❀

# PARENT TRAP.
# STUDENT TRAP.

## How to avoid dream derailers

*12/26/12 - 10:21 am*
*This log cabin is the absolute perfect place to write a book, especially because no cell phone service equals no distractions! Not to mention, we have our own log frame beds, so it's nice to sleep in peace again. Meanwhile, across the pond stands a butcher's dozen of cattle grazing down by the water. We don't see a fence anywhere, but I've never heard of a wild pack of cows. Chandler wants to ride one so he can say he did it, and he's spotted a paddleboat that could deliver us to said cow ride. "Dude, it's like our destiny!" There's a deck outside the back door but we peer through the window to keep warm. He persists, "Look! The paddleboat is pointing right at 'em! The boat beckons us, brother, and it's telling us which direction to paddle!" But from the looks of the lawless water, the wind is blowing hard today. I also can't remember ever having an "awesome time" in a paddleboat, so I tell him the grass on this side of the pond is green enough for me. Luckily, the cows and I are saved by the buzzer as it's time to write again.*

 *"White Fences" by NEEDTOBREATHE*

"One of the saddest parts of my job isn't signing off on divorce papers, it's signing off on a mortgage. In the case of the divorce, the people want free of each other and sign for their freedom. In the case of a mortgage, I have to watch people sign their death wish. They're gonna take that mortgage to the mortuary. They won't ever be free."
- Attorney who refinanced my house

# THE TRAP = SHINY STUFF

DEBT is a dream DERAILER.

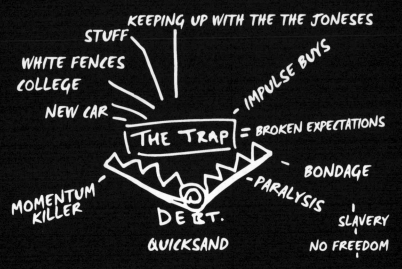

KEEPING UP WITH THE THE JONESES

STUFF

WHITE FENCES

COLLEGE

NEW CAR

IMPULSE BUYS

|THE TRAP| = BROKEN EXPECTATIONS

BONDAGE

PARALYSIS

MOMENTUM KILLER

DEBT.

QUICKSAND

SLAVERY

NO FREEDOM

STUFF       STUFF

## DO YOU OWN YOUR $, OR DOES YOUR $ OWN YOU?

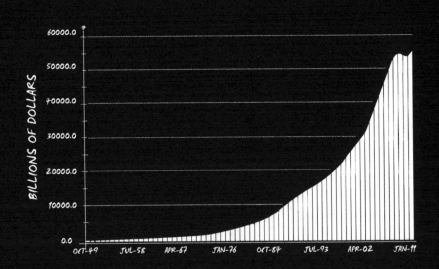

TOTAL CREDIT MARKET DEBT OWNED

SOURCE: BOARD OF GOVERNORS OF THE FEDERAL RESERVE SYSTEM/FRED

# THE DISTRACTIONS
Stop me if you've heard this one ....

"I went to college and studied _____ and it's
my dream to _____, but then _____ happened, so I
started working at _____ and I never have finished
_____. I just want what's best for my kid."

What a kid *needs* is to watch her parents break out of this broken
pattern and start living their dreams!

There are certain things you were simply born to do. Your life's
aspirations never leave you. You can push them to the back of your
mind but they will reside in your subconscious. You can put them
off for periods of time, but you're not going to be happy until you
give them the wings to fly. Unrealized potential is the most under-
diagnosed cause of depression. Stuff is the most readily available
pill on the planet for coping with this depression and distracting
yourself from thinking about your lack of flying.

## You shouldn't be using stuff to pacify an unsatisfied subconscious that's mourning the death of your unlived-life!

It's a trap! It's a trap! More stuff means more distractions, more debt,
and more disappointment. I strongly encourage you to avoid debt.
Debt will direct the flow of money against you. The pressure to buy
things you can't afford will be overwhelming. You will be profiled,
tagged, and targeted by nearly everyone you buy something from
and they will keep coming back for more.

Buy only what you can afford and pay the full price. I know it's trite,
but it bears repeating. It's difficult to keep up with the cost of living
even at the sticker price. Adding finance charges to everything
makes it impossible.

Living with a system that keeps you in the red can cost you your life. When you take on debt, the rat race begins. It's a wheel that keeps on spinning. Run your life without the distraction of debt if you want to really see the world.

# THE DISTRACTORS

I want to challenge you to look a little deeper into why you do the things you do and why you buy the things you buy. Think for a second about the things that cause you debt. Who's telling you to buy those things? Who's writing the script? Why is everyone following it?

The truth is that advertising wrote much of the script. Over time, social pressure from advertising has changed the way we function as families. Parents bought the script, and children are learning or have learned the script. According to the script, a family that shares one car isn't normal anymore. And obviously what isn't normal isn't acceptable. The script is full of broken expectations. The script is broken.

Write your own script for crying out loud! Mine says that a family that shares one car is totally normal and totally acceptable.

# IT ALL STARTS
# WITH THE FRESHMAN 15

Everyone's heard of the "Freshman 15," the weight a typical college freshman gains in his or her first year of college. Have you considered how much debt weight you're going to gain your freshman year? Consider that if you finish college with the average amount of debt, $27,750, and make the $234.17 minimum payment each month after graduation, it will take you FIFTEEN years to pay it off. And you'll have paid an additional $19,000 in interest. Even if you cut the pay-off time in half, to seven years — basically the amount of time it took you to finish all of middle school and all of high school — you'll have to find a way to come up with $405.39 every month to mail to your creditor. Imagine if that was really your reality. It easily can be. MILLIONS are in this situation. And just like "The Freshman 15" it goes on easy, but is much harder to work off.

I spoke with a senior at Furman University recently who told me his tuition bill was almost $200,000! I said "Wow! What are you going to do with your degree?" He said, "It's a fairly general degree. I don't really know what I want to do yet. Maybe I'll get my master's in something." (*Insert my jaw dropping.*)

Don't spend thousands of dollars on a general degree just because that is what everybody else is doing. Challenge what is normal. Consider your goals and your dreams and only take steps that will actually help you reach those goals and dreams.

Federal money borrowed by U.S. students to go to collage:

1977 - $7.8 billion
1989 - $12 billion
1996 - $30 billion
2009 - $70 billion

You don't have to bury yourself in debt
just to educate yourself.

There are some great alternatives to racking up debt. Consider an internship where you will gain FREE knowledge, on site, and it's real life. You can also combine internships with a year or two at a technical college. In most cases the quality of the education is the same, but the cost is a fraction.

Don't lose sight of the big picture. The purpose of college or going back to school is to launch you into a better future. Our friend from Furman could have saved $90,000 by going to the tech school down the street. A future with a $700 monthly student loan payment FOR TWENTY YEARS might as well be a set of handcuffs. Debt is the enemy of exploration. Internships aren't an option once you have a hefty debt payment every month that can't be missed. Now, imagine if you could use that money to advance your life. Be smart about the school you pick and how much money you spend while you're there.

Here are some practical tips for how to save money during your first years away from home, at school, or once you're on your own:

★ **Buy used textbooks**. They're widely available from online sites such as Half.com, AbeBooks.com, and Amazon.com. Or buy them from used bookstores at heavily discounted prices. Ask friends. You can save $100 or more per book in some cases.

★ **Save on rent**. Sometimes saving $50 on rent by living farther away from school or work isn't worth it. Be close enough to walk or bike if possible. The money you'll save on gas and parking tickets is worth it, and you get the much-needed exercise. You can also get a roommate; sharing a room or small apartment will cut your costs in half.

★ **Be the creative one!** Fun activities don't have to cost a lot of money and there are plenty of alternatives to restaurants, movie theatres, and cafes. Plan a picnic in the park or cook a meal together and invite another group over to join you. Play Frisbee golf in the park. These are a fraction of the cost and often more enjoyable!

★ **Don't try to "keep up with the Joneses."** Just because your friends or neighbors have a brand new car or a huge house doesn't mean you have to, especially if those things are outside of your budget. In the end, having a large amount of debt will cause more stress than they are worth.

★ **Shop smart.** Use coupons, store rewards programs, and sales. There is a ton of information online about how best to combine these tactics or use them separately. They can all save you a ton of money on things you need.

★ **Be smart about using the money you save.** All of the tips above are great, but won't mean anything if you don't do something smart with the extra money. Use the extra cash to pay down existing debt, open a savings account, or invest it.

# BREAKING OUT!

If there was a magic wand that could eliminate all of your debt (or your parents' debt if you're still in school):

★ Where would you live? Who would you work for? What would you do with money you save in finance charges?

If you have debt and want some good ideas for how to eliminate it, check out:

★ "The Total Money Makeover" by Dave Ramsey
★ "The Money Book for the Young, Fabulous and Broke" by Suze Orman

★     ★     ★

☙ There is strength in your freedom from debt ☙

# FORT KNOX

## Low-tech piggy banks buy the best high-tech toys

*12/26/12 - 12:45 pm*
*The nearest restaurant is 20 miles away, but luckily I grabbed some chili beans from Mom's pantry and there is a small stove here. No bowls, so I poured the hot chili back into the empty aluminum cans. Roughin' it! This reminds me of one of my all-time favorite meals, my first "foil meal." I had it on a backpacking trip with my dad before Chandler was born, and I'll never forget it. A small T-bone steak, pocket-knife-sliced potatoes, and onions camouflaged in black pepper, all wrapped in aluminum foil and placed on top of hot coals that Dad had wrangled away from the fire. It takes about half an hour for it to cook.*

*I still remember the sound of unwrapping my first foil meal dinner: the way the rising steam blanketed my cold face and the peppery smell of our coal-cooked feast flushed my campfire smoke-filled nostrils with satisfaction. Every bite was worth every bit of the wait.*

*By the way, I'm not even gonna pretend this is a cool or interesting topic. It's usually rigid and boring. I'll make it painless, but I can't skip over it because it's as powerful as it is foundational, and as profitable as it is essential.*

 *"Don't Do It" (Marvin Gaye) as covered by The Band*

## "STEWARDSHIP"

noun [ˈstü-ərd-ˌship, ˈstyü-; ˈst(y)ùrd-]
The conducting, supervising, or managing of something; especially:
the careful and responsible management of something
entrusted to one's care.

In Chapter 12, the first chapter on money, I told you that money is a force to be reckoned with. Financial mismanagement and the stress it causes can kill your hope, drive you and your loved ones apart, and worse, keep you from focusing on your life's calling.

This stress can be eliminated with what I call the 4 Pillars of Stewardship, which include saving, thrift, management, and planning.

# SAVING

My mom gave me an allowance when I was five years old. $1 per week (in dimes). She and my dad also gave me my first piggy bank, affectionately called "Fort Knox."

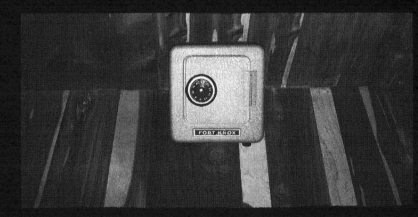

*Fort Knox is now full of grade school love letters.*
*I once made the mistake of telling Chandler. Not smart.*

10% went to God.
10% went to Fort Knox.
80% went to baseball cards.

I was the gatekeeper. Time passed. I couldn't see inside "Fort Knox," but that's the point, right? If you wait a little while before you peek inside the vault, you'll have learned the value of keeping it closed. When I was old enough to work on the construction site with my dad, he paid me to pick up trash and fetch him things. For some unknown reason (maybe it was a God thing or Mom insisting that I not waste my money), I saved *three* summers' worth of paychecks. I wasn't necessarily "saving up" for anything, but I just ... saved it. I still don't know why.

Eventually, I used the money to buy my first guitar and a tape recorder.

I remember asking permission to spend the money (*because it was more than I had ever spent!*) and my dad saying, "Ha! Why are you asking me? It's *your* money. You earned it." I like to think that I played guitar more and got more value out of my recorder because I knew how hard I had worked picking up trash and how disciplined I had been not to waste the money I had earned.

# THRIFT
In 10th grade I worried aloud to my friend Daniel about spending $.30 to add bacon to my hamburger. I wasn't asking for a handout or making a joke. I was serious. He laughed at me. I was saving money at the time for my first pair of real headphones. I was able to laugh at the situation and it probably gives you a good idea of how thrifty I had to be growing up to get the high tech toys I wanted for the recording studio I started when I was 16.

My mom introduced me to all these weird words growing up like "thrifty" and "frugal." She used to have a book called "Tightwad Gazette;" I'll never forget it. It was a dorky book for sure, but it was full of ways to feed, clothe, and provide for your family and spend only 1/3 of the money. The idea is to get by on less by using your money and resources carefully and not wastefully. My mom was a real student of thriftiness and this was a huge component to my family eliminating debt, saving for our future, and learning to be good stewards with our money and resources.

Here are some of the basic tenets of frugal living:

* **Go with a smaller car** – save on gas. Save the environment.

* **Look for used first** – whether you're buying clothes or an inkjet printer, you can save a small fortune every year by buying some things used. Shop craigslist, garage sales, or thrift shops.

* **Eat out less** – restaurants, especially nice ones, can cost 10x more than eating at home.

* **Do it yourself** – Build it! Fix it! Remodel it! If you don't know how to fix a leaky fridge, someone will proudly show you on YouTube and save you a $100 call to the repairman.

* **Use the internet** – not only is the internet a great source for finding the best deals, you can also use it to find coupons, sales, and product reviews to make sure you're getting the best bang for your buck.

* **Use your phone** – if you have a smart phone, there are a number of money-saving apps that will help you track, manage, and spend your money wisely. Some of my favorites are Groupon and mint.com.

Some of these things may strike you as "not cool" – but that's the social pressure from advertising talking! And I can testify that figuring out how to create things on your own is far more rewarding than handing over the cash for some factory-made product from China. You don't "gotta have the newest thing." And my mom is proof that you can get more of what you really want in life by trimming the fat here and there.

# MANAGEMENT

My mom wanted me to have a checkbook instead of a debit card, so that I would have to keep a ledger and have a good idea of how much I was spending. I'll never forget a note I found when I got home from school one afternoon that said "WE NEED TO TALK!!!" – cue heart racing. Oh, crap. What did she find out?! What's my story? Turns out it was because I had written a dozen checks but only entered the first one into the ledger.

Money management is the buffer between you and your bottom line.

Do you tense up when the ATM is printing your account balance? I've been there. It stinks, doesn't it? "Getting ahead" can be a really tough thing to do. My mom made it easier for me by giving me real life examples of how to do it. She has a backpack full because she and my dad were 20 (twenty!) when they got married. They truly had nothing but love and learned the hard way, so she was pretty determined to get me started on the right path.

Here are some of the best things I learned from Mom on money management:

★   Do the math. Know where your money is going. You won't get any water out of the hose if there are kinks and leaks.

★   If money is tight, you've got to make a budget.

★   Make sure your expenses aren't exceeding your income.

★   Setting financial goals will do for you what exercising does for your diet. All of a sudden you're more aware of what you're spending and you consume less.

★   Pay on time. Interest is your enemy. If you pay more for everything due to finance charges, you'll have less .... and you're an idiot. - Love, Mom

# PLANNING

I'm going to continue sharing notes from Mom since she had a thoughtful way of boiling it down for me ....

"No money down, no interest, no payments for 12 months!" – Beware of people trying to give you stuff without taking any money. They'll get their money. You'll pay dearly.

Mom suggests: "No Financing! No Interest! No Debt!" – It's called pay for it all up front with cash or with a debit card.

Emergency Fund  –  save at least $2,000 and set it aside for emergencies. This will ensure that when emergencies happen, you don't go into debt. Unforeseen expenses, like a new transmission for your car or an unexpected trip to the ER, can take a while to recover from. But you know they will happen eventually, so save for them now!

This is my number one recommendation for everyone. If you don't have an emergency fund, start saving for one. Once it's there, don't touch it!! Put it in a separate savings account so it doesn't get mixed in with your spending money. Keep it out of sight and out of mind and it will be the airbag when your next financial wreck occurs.

The next best thing you can do for planning and protecting your financial future is saving enough money to cover your expenses for three to six months. Yes, I know that's a lot of money. It took me a while to save that up for myself, but once it was there, I noticed a massive decrease in stress. I was far away from going into debt and I knew from that point on, if ever I needed to make a career change, or if I got into an accident, my bills would be paid. I wouldn't wake up in financial ruin.

Fake Zero — When people spend down to their $0.00 balance and there are several days until the next paycheck, most try to put on the brakes, try to stop spending, and brace themselves for overdraft fees, bounced checks, and trouble. One way to prevent this is to create an imaginary zero. Reassign your stop sign to a higher amount, like $500.

Pretend that's zero, so that if your cell phone bill or something you weren't expecting comes in at an odd time, you still have enough to cover it.

# BREAKING OUT!

Look at your online spending for the last 3 months. Find 3-4 things that are recurring charges for you. Now find a cheaper alternative or ask yourself if you really need it.

Additional resources ....

- ★   "Tightwad Gazette" by Amy Dacyzyn
- ★   "Think and Grow Rich" by Napoleon Hill

★      ★      ★

ᔓ There is strength in your stewardship ᔔ

# YOU, INC.

How to harness the benefits of entrepreneurship

*12/26/12 - 4:05 pm*
*Tonight is an extra special night. It's the last night*
*Chandler and I will get to spend together for a while*
*and there is a great sense of accomplishment starting*
*to bloom for both of us. It's amazing how many memories*
*from my childhood have come rushing back to me. In a*
*way I feel like if my stories were the lyrics to a song, it*
*would definitely be a country song! After years of going*
*to sleep in one city and waking up in another, it feels nice*
*to relive some of my redneck childhood. I promise all of*
*this construction workin', foil meal, campfire talk is 100%*
*real. You have my word. Oh, crap. I just remembered the*
*picture Chandler took of me sitting on a TRACTOR. My*
*adolescent years were definitely a country song!*

 *"Saw You First" by Givers*

# ENTREPRENEURSHIP IS A BEAUTIFUL THING

Buying my first guitar and a tape recorder with the money I had
saved felt awesome. I wanted to continue buying things that could
help me in the future; therefore, I continued to save my money.

When I was in high school, the idea of picking up trash and fetching
things for my dad started to lose its appeal. Instead, I wanted to
make money by recording bands. But in order to do what I really
wanted, I needed to invest in some recording equipment. Again, I
saved hard and was eventually able to get the equipment that I
needed — which I paid for in cash! With entrepreneurial wisdom
from my parents, as a junior in high school, I was making $45 an hour
doing something I loved — recording music!

Everyone in town knew that if they wanted an awesome sounding record, there was only one studio to call, Old Plantation Studios.

**MY ROOKIE CARD!**

*Earlier this week I found my first business card.*
*I still have a box of these somewhere. Why I thought I would actually*
*hand out 1,000 of these is beyond me; I betcha there's 950 unused and in*
*mint condition.*

Can you imagine how I felt the day my high school Latin teacher announced to the class, a job opening that paid $7 an hour? Minimum wage was $4.75 then, so my classmates were shocked and nearly giddy. I didn't feel smug or disdainful of that job opening, but I sure felt grateful that I was making a pretty incredible hourly rate AND doing something I was passionate about.

What I did at age 16 isn't difficult. Now, it wasn't a walk in the park by any means, but it's not out of reach for anyone willing to put in the effort. It doesn't matter if you're in high school. It doesn't matter if you're way out of college. It's not too late to start a new business that puts you in a position to do something you love and be appreciated and richly rewarded for your hard work! Do you have dreams and desires and goals for a better life? You can start making them happen today. Entrepreneurship is the way!

Tired of your boss? Fire him. Hire yourself.

If you're like me, you don't really like the idea of "falling in line." Climbing the corporate ladder isn't for you. Working in a cubicle would be placing your talent and potential inside a small box. You need room to grow — wide open space to be you. Sure, you could follow someone else's orders and do the job well, but you know you were put on this earth to do something far greater than push paper for a suit. There's no better or more freeing feeling than waking up and knowing that you can do anything you want to do. No one is telling you when to arrive, when to leave, or what to do. You make the rules, because you're the boss. The public education system was designed during the industrial revolution to produce loyal, faithful workers. It was designed to serve industrialism, so naturally it teaches you to work until you're 65.

But you're a leader, not a follower. You're capable of doing anything you set your mind to, but that's only if your mind isn't bound to conventional parameters. Keep your eyes open for opportunities to start a business that allows you to explore your passion. Entrepreneurship is a key to unlocking and freeing yourself, freeing your creativity, and freeing the growth that will come from striking out on your own.

# YOU, INC.

Let's talk about the secret that has given me thousands of dollars a year in extra capital to buy new equipment, launch new ideas, and invest in my future. Very few people know or understand this, but it's the easiest and most dynamic way to make money work for you. You're about to become your own business — actually, you already are your own business. Think about it. You have income and you pay taxes (or you soon will). You have expenses, you buy stuff. All the same things a business does ... but without the secret ingredient. If you haven't incorporated yourself then you're doing all the hard work, paying higher taxes, and receiving none of the benefits or incentives the government gives to small business owners.

**KNOW THE RULES. WIN THE GAME.** Bo Rinehart, my band mate and best friend, is a master of Scrabble. I mean a MASTER. He's studied the rulebook and the cheat sheets. He knows all the words that start with "Q". He knows all the two letter words that are only used in Scrabble. And he wins. Every. Time.

Owning your own business and knowing which tax breaks to use will help you win every time you get your tax refund. Businesses create jobs, create sales, and buy products from other businesses — all of which generates income tax and sales tax revenue for the government. To encourage people to start new businesses, the IRS gives massive tax incentives to the business owners. The basic idea is that by taxing only the profit a business earns, you give the business more capital to grow.

Let's use my first business as an example. PLANTATION STUDIOS made around $20,000 during my junior year of high school. It was my first full year of operation, my business was growing like crazy, and I spent all of the money on things that helped it grow. I bought new microphones, more headphones, cables, even raw materials from the hardware store to build an isolation booth. I bought new cymbals for my drum set. I would surprise the bands with pizza mid-way through the recording session (Thanks, Mom!).

I bought a new cell phone, business cards, furniture for the bands to sit on, and I kept every receipt. Obviously I bought lots of fun stuff with the money; I spent it all on my business. I qualified for $20,000 in tax deductions , so I paid $0 in income taxes. This is legal. I still paid sales tax on all of the stuff I bought. The people who made the stuff earn a wage that's taxed. The IRS makes their money by encouraging me, the business owner, to spend money. *Hire an awesome tax-accountant! They are worth every penny.*

Had I worked for McDonalds and made $20,000 my junior year of high school (yeah, right!), McDonalds would have automatically deducted half of that for Federal tax, State tax, Social Security, etc. You know the drill. With the $10,000 I actually got to use, most of it would've gone to the same basic expenditures (phone bill; gas, since I would've driven to work; gotten speeding tickets and higher insurance, since I'm usually running late). When all is said and done, the money I would've had left to invest in my future would've been about enough to buy just the pizza. I'd have been out of money, I wouldn't have had any new music equipment, and when it came to tax time, I wouldn't have had any deductions to claim. That's broken!

Are you seeing how opposite these scenarios are?? Which would you choose? Who in their right mind would say, "Sign me up to make someone else rich, take half my money in taxes, give me zero tax deductions, and let me do that until I'm 65!"?! That's broken! The system's motto is "Go to school, *get* a job." You need to think: "Go to school, *create* a job."

# POST-TAXES SPENDING VS. PRE-TAXES SPENDING

This is far and away the biggest advantage to incorporating yourself. If you work for a paycheck, all of your purchases are paid for post-taxes. Taxes are deducted from your check and then you buy stuff with the money that's left over (as illustrated on the left). However, if you incorporate yourself, all of your business purchases are pre-taxes; you buy stuff and then pay taxes only on the money left over. Imagine if year after year you got to reinvest $10,000 in yourself and your business. I say "yourself" because books (like this one) and trade magazines count as business expenses. Spending money to improve yourself, even going back to school, is a tax deduction because you are making your business better. Setting up your business to take advantage of all of these amazing tax incentives is easy and I'll walk you through it at the end of this chapter.

# THE POWER OF THE PIPELINE

A pipeline, by definition requires a source, a tap, and a method for delivery.

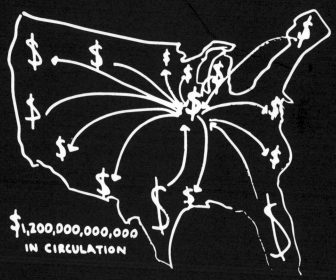

$1,200,000,000,000
IN CIRCULATION

Every day BILLIONS of dollars circulate through the hands of billions of people, both physically and electronically. It's basically a large pool of money. The money will be spent on *something*. Hot dogs. Back rubs. Sky Mall. The money is constantly flowing. It's not hard to tap into, and all you need is a simple, sturdy system to make sure it's flowing into your pocket.

Imagine for a minute you have an empty swimming pool in your backyard. Now imagine that the public road in front of your house is a freshwater mountain river with crystal clear water. One day you decide to build a channel to divert just a little bit of the water to your empty pool. You dig and dig and dig and voila! Water is flowing into your backyard swimming pool, filling it slowly. You've tapped into the source and created a method for the water to continuously flow. It doesn't take long for the pool to fill. In fact, this weekend you can have a pool party and splash all you want because the water supply is consistent!

Your monthly budget is like this swimming pool. You have to put water in so you can swim. By creating a pipeline from the river of money to your bank account, you can splash and play without worrying about running out. The work is DONE! You can retire and play all you want. You can travel and when you come back home, the pool is still full. Congratulations, you've broken out of the corporate system! You "retire" when you're young, give often and generously, and pursue all the things that you feel pulling at you. I call that **THE FREEDOM TO LIVE AND GIVE.**

Where most people go wrong is they work a full time job building someone else's pipeline. They're exchanging time for money. They don't retire until they are 65, and by then there isn't much time or energy for splashing. That's broken!

# THE FOUNDATION

A friend of mine named Dane Maxwell had several family members in the real estate business who complained frequently about the mountains of paperwork and how frustrating it is to drive back to the office just to find a paper that someone needs faxed. He created a service-based software company called Paperless Pipeline to put all the documents online and in one place. He was 24. He knew nothing about software. He knew very little about real estate. He didn't spend a dime of his own money to launch Paperless Pipeline, yet in its first month of service he was making $6,000 per month. (*Dane, if you're reading this, thanks for giving your company a name that works serendipitously well with my pipeline analogy! Ha!*)

How did he do it? He interviewed 100 real estate agents and listened. He said, "I'm building a software program that aims to fix your problems. What problems can it fix for you?"

The agents designed the product for him. Then he went to three software developers and said, "If you were to design this, what would it look like?" They, in turn, gave him a sketch of what the interface would look like (for free) and he showed them to the agents and they gave him wonderful feedback about what they liked and disliked about each one. Dane didn't start with a product. He started with a customer! Then he got his potential customers to build the product for him!! Then Dane said, "How much time would this software save you?" to which they replied, "Oh my, probably 10-15 hours a month!" The conversation continued a little something like this:

🂱🂱 Dane: "And how much is an hour of your time worth?"

Agent: "Probably $50. At least."

Dane: "Wow. So that's between $500 and $750. What about the physical savings? Gas, wear and tear on your car from driving back and forth to the office, and printing expenses?"

Agent: "Probably another $250."

Dane: "So the software will save you $750 to $1,000 every month and obviously make keeping track of all the documents much easier. How much would you pay for that if it were a monthly service?"

HE DIDN'T HAVE TO GUESS THE VALUE OF HIS PRODUCT. HE ASKED THE POTENTIAL CUSTOMERS!! Wow. Most of them said "around $100." Of the first 100 he interviewed, 60 agreed to the monthly fee. 60 customers? That's not a lot. $100? That's not a lot either. $6,000 showing up in the mailbox every month?? That's a lot!

It gets better.

Many of the agents agreed to help him pay for the software development and in turn he gave them 10% off for life. Dane invested $0 in the company. He started with the customer, asked them exactly what they needed, and they paid to develop it.

It gets even better. This took 8 weeks.

If Dane worked for a software company, he would be in the trenches month after month, building software and using the broken job model of exchanging time for money. Instead, he built a pipeline.

Paperless Pipeline delivers $40,000 a month in passive income and is growing! He spends zero hours per month working on his pipeline. And now he's teaching other people how to do what he did from start to finish in a roundtable class called The Foundation. Chandler just finished recently and it's the best thing going right now. If you aren't sure where you want to go to college, or if you're looking for a career change that will pay dividends *ad infinitum*, go to www.thefoundation.com

# HOW TO START A SMALL BUSINESS IN A FEW HOURS

The steps required to register your business with the IRS, state, and local government are actually really simple. Don't be afraid. Even though you are "applying" for approval with each, they have no reason to deny you. They want you to register so they can collect any applicable taxes. At the state and local level they will also check to make sure there isn't already a business by the same name you're submitting.

**1. Apply for an Employment Identification Number (EIN) from the IRS.** That takes about ten minutes and you will likely be approved. You can only apply during their business hours. (Currently 7am to 10pm Eastern Time, Monday through Friday.)

**2. Select a business structure.**

* Sole proprietorship
* Partnership
* Corporation
* S-Corporation
* Limited Liability Company (LLC)

Definitions of each can be found here. This will take 15 minutes tops. www.goo.gl/z9rfVr

**3. Register your business with the state.** Google "Articles of Incorporation" along with the name of your state. Most likely your Secretary of State has a website (*unless you live in Mississippi or something. Boom! Roasted!*).

There you'll find the necessary forms. You'll print these, complete and sign, and mail in the fee (usually around $100) along with a self-addressed, stamped envelope. This will take 20 minutes to complete.

Expect to wait 4-6 weeks for a response. You'll get a certificate from the state that will be signed by the Secretary of State and notarized with a fancy state seal.

**4. Register your business with the county.** It's best to do this in person at the County Clerk's office. This usually costs around $50 per year and takes 15 minutes.

So not as fun as a YouTube video binge, but you can knock this out in an afternoon!

*"Please don't sue me" disclaimer: If you're not sure what's best for your business, you may want to consult an attorney to make sure that you form your business correctly.*

*Additional resources:*
★ *"Rich Dad, Poor Dad" by Robert Kiyosaki*

*Watch this two-minute video! Robert Kiyosaki also does a masterful job of explaining why, if you work for a paycheck, you'll be in the highest tax bracket. www.boltbros.com/videos*

# BREAKING OUT!

Incorporate yourself, start a new career on the side, and start taking advantage of enormous tax savings! Don't be intimidated. You can do it.

★ It doesn't matter how small, silly, or unconventional your product is. If it's sock puppets that you plan on selling, you can still write off googley eyes.

★ It doesn't matter how much you sell, if anything, in your first year. You can claim deductions that will benefit you come April 15th.

★ Stop paying taxes on all your work-related expenses!

Owning a business is an adventure. Be your own boss. Do something you're passionate about. Create jobs for others. Pass on a legacy to your kids. Set your own schedule. Cut the commute. Unlock your creativity. Start your own business!

★          ★          ★

## ∽ There is strength in your financial education ∾

# ✑ BEDTIME STORY ✑

*End of Day 6 - 12:52 am FIIIIIIREWOOOOOOORKS!*
*We lit 'em all. Burned down every sparkler too. Oh, what a night!*
*The moon was full and shining brightly off the pond. The water's*
*reflection really amplified the fireworks! Quite a show and I didn't*
*light any bales of hay on fire with Roman candles this year! ... well,*
*New Year's Eve is in five days, so that hay ain't in the clear, yet!*
*It's really cold outside, especially up here in the Carolina mountains,*
*but lucky for us this vintage cabin has a modern hot tub! What, you*
*didn't think we were totally roughin' it out here, did ya?*

*This is the good life ....*
*Steam rising off the perfectly*
*temperatured 103 degree water ....*
*Bubbles on high ....*
*Starry night sky ....*
*On top of the mountain ....*

*Chandler and I felt like kings tonight.*
*Our first real vacation, just the two*
*of us. Okay, so we worked like mad*
*men the entire trip, but tonight was*
*the exhale.*

# NIGHTCAP

## DAY 6: YOUR MONEY

★ Money is a force to be reckoned with ★

★ Indifference is not an option ★

★ You can direct the flow of money if you know how it works ★

★ Make it to give it away ★

★ In giving, although it doesn't seem so, you receive ★

★ Debt is a dream derailer ★

★ Secure your financial future using the 4 Pillars of Stewardship ★
Saving, Thrift, Management, and Planning

★ The secret of The Pipeline starts with You, Inc. and will ★
give you the freedom to live and give

★ Know the rules. Win the game ★

★ Pre-Tax money goes farther. Invest in You, Inc. ★
THEN pay taxes only on profit

★ Don't waste your adult life exchanging time for money; Build a pipeline ★

# DAY 7

## THE END
## & NEW BEGINNINGS

*12/27/12 - 9:50 am*
*It's day 7 and the end of one of the best weeks of my life.*
*We've driven across the state of South Carolina three*
*times:*

★ *from my home in Charleston to the house we grew up in*
   *(where we started writing the book),*

★ *down to Edisto Island, where my family always*
   *vacations,*

★ *then back to the Smokey Mountains, to a remote cabin*
   *(where we're out of real food, but getting by on coffee*
   *dregs and what's left of the peanut butter).*

*My brother is cooler than he's ever been and I'm excited*
*knowing that the future is bright for both of us; and is*
*surely its brightest when we work together.*

*Remember how "MANY mini Successes" build confidence? I*
*just realized that this book, no matter how many people*
*read it, is a mini success for me because I completed the task*
*without giving up! I beat my procrastination! I overcame*
*perfectionism! Chandler put us on the clock and we met our*
*deadline. We wrote every chapter together.*

*I still have no idea what he's written, but I can't wait to read it on the day the book is released.*

*Recalling the pivotal lessons of my childhood has proven to be an emotional trek down memory lane. I was prepared to laugh at the funny stories, but I didn't anticipate tears of gratitude. Retracing my footsteps in the sand led me to milestone after milestone of a great love that I'm not sure I even understand. Perhaps I will when I have children of my own. The realization that two normal people created 18 years full of exceptional wisdom and examples of sacrifice was simply overwhelming at times. What have I done that can compare to this? Nothing. The debt I owe my parents is one I can never repay. It is my hope that through retelling their lessons, I can make them live forever. They certainly deserve eternity.*

 *"L'estasi dell'oro" by Ennio Morricone*

# THE NEW SYSTEM

**Your Mindset.** We are creatures of habit that organize life with systems. But it's okay to be different and take a unique path. YOU can break out of a broken system by creating your own, NEW system. Today is the day. Action is required. Indifference is not an option.

**Your Actions.** Stop procrastinating, simplify, and work your butt off.

**Your Influences.** You are influenced by the people around you — surround yourself with people who support and encourage you. Equally as important is your ability to change other people's lives. Share your gifts and talents — they aren't yours to keep to yourself!

**Your Momentum.** Failure is a chance to learn and grow. Things that seem like roadblocks to your success are actually opportunities for you to grow. People don't plan to fail, they fail to plan. Make your plan today so that you spend the rest of your life chasing and embracing all the big dreams, experiences, and passions swirling around inside of you.

**Your Money.** You'll reap endless benefits from giving your money away. Avoid debt and maintain the four pillars of stewardship.

**You, Inc.** The only thing stopping you from realizing your dreams is the broken system. Invest in yourself. Change your patterns, and break out! You can do this!

---

*I had a really great heart to heart with Chandler last night. We recapped this crazy week-long journey and dreamt aloud about a future of working together. We proved a lot to each other this week. He doesn't feel like "just my little brother" anymore. We're equal. We work together exceptionally well even though we're very different.*

*We addressed some of our personal fears moving forward. It's one thing to bare your soul to a pack of black construction paper; it's another to release it to the world. A part of me is scared to death. Chandler reminded me last night that my passion and desire to help people is a stronger force than fear. He's a wise man. It feels like we're entering a season of closeness that we have never experienced before. He's no longer my little brother; he's my friend.*

*I hope every year has a week like this.*

*One final P.S...*

*I cannot thank you enough for allowing me to share this unforgettable week with you. I would love to hear what you took away from these stories. Share your thoughts with me on twitter @drsethbolt. I also want to thank you for purchasing this book and for telling your friends about it. Chandler and I will be making a donation on your behalf to Palmetto Medical Initiative. 100% of this book's profit will be given to charity.*

*Thank you for making a difference!*

# BREAKING OUT
## OF A BROKEN CYCLE

---

Roughly one year after writing the book, I find myself reading back through this one-week journey — allowing all the memories to come flooding back and reflecting on life's lessons. This past year was a tough one but I'm growing and changing because of it. I cannot help but feel that I've gained a better, slightly different perspective on how very relevant my parent's lessons really are. So, if you'd be so kind, allow me to share what I've learned this past year in regard to success and happiness.

---

*3/28/14 1:35 am*
*Success ≠ Happiness*
*Historically, feelings of being successful and happy have both been short-lived for me, whether in my primary job as the bass player for NEEDTOBREATHE or any of the numerous projects I do in my free time.*

*Let me explain: I would experience happiness following the success of a project, but since that happiness didn't last very long I would start a new project immediately in order to get the feeling of happiness back again. This past year I realized that I have filled my time and my life with projects to the point that I have blocked out nearly everything (and everyone) else, and I had to stop and ask myself why. Why would I decline phone calls from my mother, whose time and attention are precious, in order to stay focused on one of my silly projects?*

*Why would I avoid social functions that guarantee laughter and quality conversation? Why do I keep creating projects for myself that perpetuate this negative behavior?*

*I realized that my mind's algorithm for achieving happiness had a critical flaw, and consequently the engine that was driving me to be successful was also driving me crazy. I was starting each project hoping its success would bring me happiness, but there are three obvious flaws to this formula:*

1. *If the project's success didn't meet my hopes, I was not happy.*

2. *If the project's success met my expectations, I was happy - but only for a very small percentage of my overall time (most of my projects are big ones that require a lot of time to complete).*

3. *Like the cartoon carrot on a stick, happiness was in sight but slightly out of reach because it lay on the other side of my next success — but success was a moving target.*

*Sadly, this had been my formula for happiness my entire life and I didn't even realize it! I was living in a state of discontentment, seeking happiness from success and "living" a very, very busy life. I was working constantly - rarely eating a meal without "doing something productive" as I chewed, opting to work on my days off, checking email or social media during time that should be spent focused on my family and friends ... the list goes on and on. The lines between working and living became blurry. Being a "workaholic" was a badge I wore for many years but now I regret overworking. I regret missing family time and what overworking has taken away from my relationships with people who mean the world to me.*

>

*I realize that throughout my twenties I had every reason to be the happiest guy in the world, but I didn't feel that way. Now I realize the expectations I put on success were unrealistic ... and foolish. If I could go back to the 18-year old self who marched triumphantly out the doors of high school, I would tell myself three things about happiness and success:*

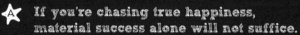 **If you're chasing true happiness, material success alone will not suffice.**

*You will not find long-term happiness in material or financial success. Certainly, you have to be able to feed, clothe, and shelter yourself — but once you're beyond the minimum, you will find that additional money will not necessarily increase your happiness.*

**True happiness doesn't happen from the outside in.**

*It starts inside of you; it starts with accepting that you are broken and imperfect, and that no amount of self-help can fix you. Happiness isn't a physical thing; it's an emotional and spiritual thing. No amount of ANY physical thing — houses, cars, business cards featuring fancy job titles, plaques for generous charitable contributions, massive retirement savings accounts or any amount of cash — none of those things can guarantee long term happiness. Allow God's unconditional love to be the basis of your self-worth and there you will find true, sustainable happiness.*

**Chasing a dream can be hard work, but catching the dream is totally worth the effort.**

*The primary lessons in this book can give you access to a successful life, make your dreams more attainable, and make life less stressful. I encourage you to seek life-balance as well, recognizing that we all need more than productivity and success (even success in reaching our dreams) to live happy, fulfilled lives. We need faith and we need people who feed our souls.*

*After experimenting with this new philosophy for six months now, I can report that I am now much happier. I no longer feel tightly wound. I have meaningful conversations for long periods of time without feeling the urge to look at my phone or feeling guilty about not working constantly. This new perspective allows me to continue living my dreams and working towards new goals — and to be happy with myself, happy with this step and the next, happy to be free, happy to be on this journey, and happy before I reach the next destination.*

# CHANDLER'S SIDE
# OF THE STORIES

# CHANDLER'S SIDE OF THE STORIES

## DAY 1 - 12/21/12 - YOUR MINDSET

## DAY 2 - 12/22/12 - YOUR ACTIONS

## DAY 3 - 12/23/12 - YOUR INFLUENCE

## DAY 4 - 12/24/12 - YOUR MOMENTUM

## DAY 5 - 12/25/12 - CHRISTMAS DAY

## DAY 6 - 12/26/12 - YOUR MONEY

## DAY 7 - 12/27/12 - BRINGING IT FULL CIRCLE

# DAY 1

## YOUR MINDSET

---

# CHAPTER 1

# CHALLENGING THE STATUS QUO

## - RIDICULOUSLY DIFFERENT -

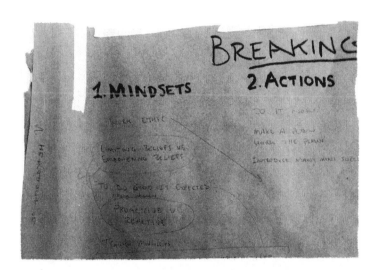

*12/21/12 - 10:55 am*
*I'm looking up at the wall where we've taped our Success*
*Map and realizing that I've got a lot of writing to do. We've*
*already got a name for the book and some good direction,*
*so it's time to get started. Lettt's gooooooo! Feeling good.*

# REBELLION IS A GOOD THING

As far back as I can remember, I've had a rebellious spirit. In fact, I was even born in a rebellious way. I was born 9-½ years after my brother, who swears that I was a "surprise."

A year before my mom gave birth to me, she had a miscarriage. I can't even imagine how tough that was for her, but it didn't diminish her desire to have a second child. A couple of months into her pregnancy with me, she experienced the same complications as the pregnancy that had ended in a miscarriage. After many sleepless nights for Mom and Dad and tons of prayer from their family and friends, I made it out ok. Well … except for my watermelon-sized head. It was so big that they thought there was something wrong with me. I couldn't sit up or walk without falling head first for the first couple years of my life. (But that's another story.) I'd like to think that it was my rebellious spirit fighting like hell during this time, refusing to go down without a fight. I still have the same rebellious attitude today that made me a fighter from Day 1.

---

"You have to leave the city of your comfort and go into the wilderness of your intuition. What you'll discover will be wonderful. What you'll discover is yourself."
– Alan Alda

---

All of our lives, we are trained to believe that rebellion is a bad thing. From early childhood on, many of our most passionate ambitions and dreams are whittled away by well-meaning parents and teachers, and a society that believes it's in our best interest to conform to fairly rigid definitions of what "success" looks like and how to achieve it. Unfortunately, this insistence on conformity has trained people to embrace mediocrity and be like everyone else.  It tends to dumb-down our dreams and our expectations of what is possible. Because of this, what we believe we can do shrinks over time. I call this the Belief Funnel.

As a child, the possibilities are endless. But as you attend school, get a job, and eventually retire, the world's expectations and beliefs about you shrink your belief in what you're capable of doing.

You weren't born to be mediocre. No one was. As a young child with dreams, you weren't thinking about what was "realistic." "Thinking realistically" happens only after you've had your dreams watered down.

Refuse to submit to this belief funnel and your mind will be opened to the abundance of possibilities you have.

---

"The only thing that interferes
with my learning is my education."
- Albert Einstein

---

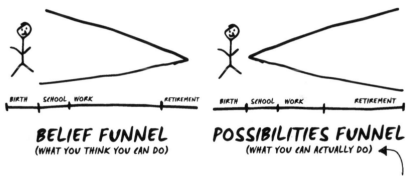

BIRTH   SCHOOL  WORK                    RETIREMENT      BIRTH   SCHOOL  WORK          RETIREMENT

## BELIEF FUNNEL           POSSIBILITIES FUNNEL
### (WHAT YOU THINK YOU CAN DO)         (WHAT YOU CAN ACTUALLY DO) ←

### THIS IS WHAT LIFE SHOULD REALLY LOOK LIKE

As we grow older and mature, our abilities are constantly improving. With the combination of our education and experience, we have the ability to accomplish more than ever. But because of the shrinking belief funnel, we often dismiss these possibilities as "unrealistic."

# BATMAN UNDERWEAR, SHOW-AND-TELL

All throughout school, I was the rowdy kid who talked too much and always got into trouble because of it. In second grade, I was having a particularly hard time with a teacher who was constantly annoyed with my excessive talking and rowdiness. Every day my mom would come to pick me up only to hear about what I'd done wrong that day. I remember one day in particular ....

Every Friday we had Show-and-Tell, (where you bring in something really awesome from home, such as your favorite toy, and show the class). Well, it just so happened that on this Friday, I forgot to bring something. In an act of desperation I reached in my backpack for the only thing I had — my spare pair of Batman-themed underwear.

I proceeded to put them on my head and proclaimed to the class: "Sometimes ... when I'm at home ... I put my underwear on my head and run around the house like this!" Then I ran around the room flailing my arms in the air and screaming. Although this was a class favorite, it didn't make my teacher very happy.

This was included in my daily "bad news" report to my mom, but all she could do was laugh. She was used to these kinds of reports after raising Seth, who, believe it or not, was the even rowdier one.

I wasn't old enough at the time, but eventually, I realized (after SEVERAL more instances like this) that I didn't really understand what school was all about, much less what I was doing there.

For lots of kids, school encourages mediocrity. This is especially true if you're different from the kind of kids schools were designed for — kids who are academically oriented; who work well with rules and structure at a young age; who have long attention spans; who are highly self-motivated and fairly compliant (in other words ... not me).

But like me, some kids who aren't A+ students (who don't work well with rules and structure, who have A.D.D.-driven attention spans; and who like to do things their own way), end up being extremely successful out in the real world ... which is why you sometimes see a well-educated person working for a college dropout ... or working for a company owned by a college dropout!

If you don't do well in school, you're scolded and punished. If you get creative and take a different route on a project, you're often "rewarded" with a bad grade. By focusing on conformity and uniformity, schools often extinguish creativity, exploration, free-thinking, and discovery. Yet those are some of the best traits of highly successful people!

After being trained this way, we're scared to make mistakes. We're scared to do anything different for fear that it might lead to a bad grade or other negative consequences. Being different is discouraged and punished, yet being mediocre is accepted.

# FAILURE IS AN OPTION!

During my freshman year of high school I had an itch to get into the investment world. The quickest and most sexy route for me was the stock market. It was such a mysterious thing, but I knew ... I wanted in! I talked to my parents about it but was quickly vetoed by my Dad (aka Mr. Play-it-Safe).

I decided to do it anyway, but I wasn't old enough to sign up for a Scottrade (stock trading) account, so I did what any ninth-grader would do.

I somehow conned my mom into helping me open an account and proceeded to dump in most of my life savings. My trading career began as I "researched" all of my options and started mindlessly purchasing stock. Unfortunately for me, it was February of 2008 and the stock market was headed for major decline. Over the next few months, my $1,500 investment was cut in half to about $750.

This was a tough pill to swallow, but this stock market debacle taught me so many things that I would've never learned if I had taken no for an answer and decided to play it safe. Not only did I learn how to make better stock buying decisions, but I also learned that failing wasn't that bad. I was so scared of losing my money when I started but for $750, I learned so many things about the stock market and about myself that I wouldn't have otherwise.

The best learning moments in life are when we fail. If you never fail, you'll never accomplish anything worth talking about. Think of the people whom you admire most. How many times do you think they've failed in their lives? Probably more than they can remember. These people are successful because they have challenged the status quo and have been rebellious enough to do things differently and risk failure.

That's what this book is all about. **Being successful and accomplishing your dreams does not depend on how smart or skilled you are.** At their core, being successful and accomplishing your dreams are about discovering your differences and unique talents and putting them to work toward the goals that are important to you. Rebellion is a good thing. A willingness to question other people's assumptions and expectations and the courage to do things differently are the traits that will help you break out of a broken system and break into the life you dream of.

I'll end this chapter with one more story. One of my favorite sports as a kid was basketball. Lots of the guys on my team had more money than I did, and their parents would spend money on camps and coaching so that their kids had the best-looking shot in the game. My shot, on the other hand, looked painful. To be honest, it looked about as funny as my watermelon-sized head. But … in spite of my crappy shot, I was the one getting all of the playing time. Because I was different. My coaches called me "scrappy" because I would outhustle, outwork, and outplay the competition at all costs. The difference between me and the other kids was my ability to hustle and my willingness to put forth effort. That determination filled a void that no amount of money or pretty shot could fill.

Rebellion IS a good thing. It's about not letting others define you and your options. It's about questioning the status quo. It's about being willing to fail and knowing that your failures will make you much stronger. It's about realizing that you can change the things around you and make them better.

# BREAKING OUT!

Think back to when you were in grade-school. List three things about yourself that made you "different" from other kids before you were 10 years old.

★ _____

★ _____

★ _____

Choose three family members or friends who knew you before you were 10 years old. Ask them what unique characteristics they noticed in you as a young kid. What made you different or set you apart from other kids your age?

**PERSON**                    **WHAT WAS UNIQUE
                              OR DIFFERENT ABOUT ME?**

_____


_____


_____


Reflect on your life now. How have the differences listed above helped you in school or work? How have they given you an advantage over your peers, colleagues, or competition?

# LIMITING BELIEFS VS. EMPOWERING BELIEFS

## - KILLING FEAR & EMBRACING FAILURE -

*12/21/12 - 1:30 pm*
*Had to go to a different room to write the first chapter.*
*Seth was playing music and I'm just too A.D.D. to write*
*with music on. This time I think I'm gonna go up to my*
*room to write — while standing up. Maybe that'll get some*
*blood flowing to my brain.*

"It's the repetition of affirmations that
leads to belief. And once that belief becomes a deep
conviction, things begin to happen."
-Muhammad Ali

Mindsets and beliefs are always working and controlling our lives from behind the scenes. They are a part of our everyday lives whether we like it or not. The beliefs that we have about ourselves and the world make us the individuals we are. Ultimately, it is our beliefs that shape our mindsets and our mindsets that shape our future. In the words of singer/songwriter Gavin DeGraw: "Belief makes things real." What we believe about ourselves has a direct impact on the things that happen to us and how we handle things that are out of our control. When a person finds a way to control his own beliefs, he's found a way to control his destiny.

At any point in our life, our beliefs are either moving us forward or sending us backward. The problem is that so many people have what I call a scarcity mindset. They see life as this thing that's really tough to conquer. They live as though there's not enough money and success to go around. These people feel as if they need to step on you to get to the top.

Most of humanity has decided that "barely making it" is acceptable. They believe that there isn't enough of all the good stuff to go around and tell themselves they'll never make it — so they settle for what they have. They bring this scarcity mindset into their everyday lives. This has become the norm and thus we have millions of people barely getting by or not getting by at all. Life doesn't have to be so hard!

The opposite of a scarcity mindset is having an abundance mindset. This is the belief that there's plenty to go around. This is the mindset of winners.

Let me give you an example. A few years ago my Mom went into real estate at one of the worst times ever. It was during the real estate crash in 2008 and real estate agents were dropping like flies. Most of the agents who survived were scratching and clawing for any remaining business. They were doing the types of things that sometimes give real estate agents a bad rap, like constantly cutting each other down. They thought there wasn't enough business for everyone, so they had to be ruthless — classic case of a scarcity mindset.

When my mom became an agent, she went to work for a national, well-known company. With no previous experience, she became #1 in her office during her first year!! Her abundance mentality led her to do anything she could to help homebuyers and agents alike. She was able to stand out as someone who was not only trustworthy, but an effective agent.

# FEAR

Fear of failure keeps us from bucking the system. It keeps us from exploring the what-ifs in life and developing our strengths, talents, and interests in ways that are different from the norm. It causes us to avoid making the painful decisions that could better our life. This is also why a lot of people spend their 50 years of hard labor living for the weekends and chasing the carrot of enjoyment that they think will come when they retire.

Author Steven Pressfield says: "If you're paralyzed with fear, it's a good sign. Fear is good. Like self-doubt, fear is an indicator. It shows you what you have to do. The more scared we are of a work or calling, the more sure we can be that we have to do it." It's fear that keeps people from pushing themselves, from believing that they can break out of a broken system, and from doing what they desperately need to do.

Doing the things that you fear causes uncertainty. This is to be expected. After all, humans are wired to react to fear and to alleviate the source.

But the times in life when we experience the most success usually follow the times when we experience a lot of uncertainty. During the uncertainty, we need to push through the paralysis of fear to reach the success waiting on the other side. Pushing past fear is difficult, but you'll find out how in the chapters to come.

# TWO TYPES OF BELIEFS

There are two types of beliefs: Limiting Beliefs and Empowering Beliefs. A Limiting Belief is a belief based in fear. It is a made-up, self-sabotaging notion that keeps you from taking action toward your dreams and desires. Your mind makes up Limiting Beliefs to avoid doing uncomfortable or scary tasks. Limiting Beliefs can also come in the form of the incorrect assumptions and expectations of others that you have accepted as truth. Here are some examples of Limiting Beliefs that you're probably familiar with.

| LIMITING BELIEFS | EMPOWERING BELIEFS |
| --- | --- |
| I'm too young and inexperienced for people to take me seriously. | |
| I don't deserve success. | |
| I'm nobody special and I'm not an "expert." | |
| Starting a business is risky and requires you to give up family and friends to succeed. | |
| If I try that, I'll probably fail and look stupid. | |
| I can't be more successful than my parents. They won't love me anymore. | |
| I don't have enough money to do that. | |
| I'm not 100% sure I'm heading in the right direction. | |
| I'm too old to "start over." | |
| I should be content with what I have, instead of focusing on what I don't. | |

Do any of these sound familiar? If so, I'm right there with ya. At some point in our lives, we've all been able to relate with at least one of these! Sometimes these beliefs are obvious because we say them to ourselves, either out loud or in our heads, all the time. Other times they're buried so deep inside of us that we don't realize how much they're affecting our decisions. Becoming aware of the Limiting Beliefs working in our minds is the first step toward defeating and eliminating them. Next we need to reverse them and change them into Empowering Beliefs.

Empowering beliefs do exactly that; they empower you! An Empowering Belief feeds your confidence and drives you forward in times of hardship. Empowering Beliefs encourage you to take control of the obstacles in your path. Here are those same Limiting Beliefs, but turned into Empowering Beliefs.

| LIMITING BELIEFS | EMPOWERING BELIEFS |
|---|---|
| I'm too young and inexperienced for people to take me seriously. | Because I'm young, I can outperform the low expectations that others often set for me. |
| I don't deserve success. | I add intrinsic value to the world. |
| I'm nobody special and I'm not an "expert." | I may not be an "expert" yet, but every "expert" started from somewhere. |
| Starting a business is risky and requires you to give up family and friends to succeed. | The people who matter to me and care about me WANT me to succeed. |
| If I try that, I'll probably fail and look stupid. | I know there's a chance for failure, but I'm fine with it because I know I'll learn so much from it. |
| I can't be more successful than my parents. They won't love me anymore. | I can't wait to make my parents proud by showing them everything I can do! |
| I don't have enough money to do that. | Money doesn't hold me back. I'll figure out a way to make it happen. |
| I'm not 100% sure I'm heading in the right direction. | Moving in the wrong direction is better than being paralyzed by fear and going nowhere. |
| I'm too old to "start over." | Because I'm older, I have the benefit of experience to help me. |
| I should be content with what I have, instead of focusing on what I don't. | People who are truly happy don't put limits on their dreams. |

# BREAKING OUT!

What are some of *your* Limiting Beliefs? Choose from the previous list or come up with some of your own and write them down.

This is not a 2 minute exercise. You're probably going to have to sit and think about this one for a little bit.

_____

_____

_____

_____

Are you sure you thought about it ...? Did you just write something down really fast?

If you're like me you probably said: *"That's a cool exercise. I'll do it later. I just want to keep reading."*

Seriously. Take a few minutes and think about this one.

How can you change those Limiting Beliefs into Empowering Beliefs? Write the "empowered" version of the beliefs here.

_____

_____

_____

_____

★     ★     ★

# CHAPTER 3

# UNLOCKING YOUR POTENTIAL

## - BRING BACK YOUR INNER 5 YEAR-OLD -

*Found this picture and trophy from a
Wal-Mart crawl-a-thon. As always, Seth takes the credit
and says that he "trained me" for it. I don't know who's
more proud, him or me.*

### 12/21/12 - 4:00 pm
Just ate some of my Mom's legendary Santa Fe Soup after
finishing the last chapter. She and Dad went to Edisto for
vacation so she cooked up a bunch of it to keep us from
having to cook. She knows us too well!

The weird thing about our potential is that it often gets hidden. It gets covered up by our doubt, by our failures, and by the discouragement we get from others. When this happens, we forget that the potential exists. It often takes a friend or coach to remind us of our potential and to kick us into action.

# BE THE BIGGEST LOSER

Growing up, one of my mom's favorite shows was The Biggest Loser. This show is a classic example of a coach bringing people to their potential. Contestants are overweight and live very unhealthy lifestyles. Inevitably, they say the reason they haven't made changes is because they don't have the willpower, time, etc., etc., to do it on their own. Trainers Bob and Jillian then teach them not only how to lose massive amounts of weight and live a healthy lifestyle, but they also motivate them to trust in their own capabilities and help them unlock potential that they didn't know they had.

Their transformations are amazing. In some cases, contestants lose over 100 pounds. I'm pretty sure they would tell you that if someone had asked them before the show if such amazing transformation was possible for them, they would have said no way. But they did it. They had the potential the whole time — they just didn't know how to use it.

There's potential inside all of us that we don't even know exists. Discovering that potential starts with opening your mind and going back to your childhood. Thinking like a child allows you to uncover the beliefs, abilities, and innate talents that have been shoved aside until now. Some of these abilities and talents are the strengths we would've kept developing if the world hadn't told us to straighten up and get in a single-file line just like everybody else.

When you uncover your unique qualities, you'll be inspired to dream bigger and reach higher.

# ACT LIKE A 5 YEAR-OLD

Thinking like a 5 year-old means ignoring your doubts and negative feedback from others. Five year-olds don't pay attention when someone says they might not play in the NBA *and* be a police officer or that they can't really be a princess when they grow up. They don't let other people's disbelief affect their dreams. As I said earlier, it means refusing to "think realistically." When you're too dumb to know you can't do something, innocence and naiveté often allow you to plow ahead, pushing through any obstacles. You make it happen because your mind doesn't let you come up with excuses.

THIS IS WHAT UNLOCKING YOUR INNER
5 YEAR-OLD LOOKS LIKE.
PRETTY EXCITING, RIGHT?

One of the more recent times I tapped into my inner child was when I was 18 years old. With the help of a mentor and an amazing internship, I decided to start my own business. I set my sights on creating and running a business with a goal of earning over $100k in revenue. This was a very 5-year-old-like goal, as it had only been done once in company history. Technically, it wasn't "realistic." In fact, when I shared my goal with friends and classmates, I received blank stares in return. The more I talked about my goal, the more people kept listing reasons why I wouldn't be able to reach it.

By unlocking my inner-child, I allowed myself to dream big, and this compelled me to trust myself and conquer the Limiting Beliefs that were holding me back. By renewing my mindset, I was able to start up and run that $100k business — and win the title of Entrepreneur of the Year by outselling and out-producing over 200 candidates.

**DREAMING BIGGER**

**UNLOCKING YOUR INNER 5 YEAR-OLD**

**TAKING ACTION**

**CONQUERING LIMITING BELIEFS**

A big reason I was able to unlock my inner-child is because my family was so supportive. They genuinely believed in what I was doing and encouraged me along the way. My parents were my biggest supporters, making me believe I could do whatever I wanted.

Not everyone can look to their family for support and not everyone has supportive people around them. It's impossible to thrive if you're surrounded by negative people (doubters). In a later chapter, I'll talk about how to get rid of the naysayers and surround yourself with positive influences that will help you thrive.

# TURN THE BELIEF AROUND

In the previous chapter, we saw how important it is to change Limiting Beliefs into Empowering Beliefs. Conquering Limiting Beliefs can be tough to do, but when you finally eliminate them, you'll be amazed at all the extra potential you unlock.

The root of all Limiting Beliefs lies in false statements that past experience has forced our subconscious to accept as true. These false beliefs can often be traced back to a painful failure or bad memory from childhood.

In order to reverse strong Limiting Beliefs, it helps to funnel them through this framework. (Original source & inspiration by Byron Katie.)

**1.** Is this belief true? (Yes or no. If no, move to question 3.)

**2.** Is this belief true without a shadow of a doubt? (Yes or no.)
   Is there any way you could prove this belief to be wrong?

**3.** How do you feel when considering this belief?

★   Does it bring peace or stress into your life?

★   What physical sensations and emotions arise when you believe the thought? Allow yourself to experience them now.

★   What images do you see, of your past and your future, when you believe the thought?

★   What obsessions or addictions begin to rise to the surface when you believe the thought? (Do you act out with unhealthy distractions like alcohol, drugs, credit cards, food, sex, television?)

**4.** How do you treat yourself and others when you believe the thought?

**5.** Who or what are you without the thought?

**6.** What would the opposite thought be?

**7.** How do you feel when considering this opposite thought?

What did this exercise reveal to you? The Breaking Out exercise at the end of this chapter will help you analyze the results of running your belief through this framework.

By changing beliefs from Limiting to Empowering, you're well on your way to making a true change. Battling Limiting Beliefs is an ongoing process. Just when you think that you've reversed a belief for good, the old belief will rear its head again. Expect that this will happen, and be prepared for it — but don't be alarmed. You have the tools to move past it.

Even while experiencing success running my business, Limiting Beliefs occasionally crept back into my head and slowed my progress. I remember being two-thirds of the way through my summer when Limiting Beliefs brought me to my lowest of lows.

Business was going poorly and I was really frustrated. I was away from my friends and family during this time and I wanted to give up. It was the first time since I started the business that I thought I might not reach my goals. I finally recognized the funk I was in and forced myself to reverse the Limiting Beliefs that were keeping me down. This was a slow, difficult process, but it helped me rebound from my momentary failure and sprint to the finish line.

Here's what the reversal of a couple of my Limiting Beliefs looks like:

| LIMITING BELIEF | EMPOWERING BELIEF | ACTION TAKEN |
|---|---|---|
| I'm a bad manager. | I'm a much better manager now that I've learned from my mistakes. I need a fresh start so I can prove myself. | I hired a new crew and changed my management style. This created a much better culture for my team. |
| I guess I'm not good enough to be the best in the country. | I am the best in the country and I'll prove it by consistently working harder and smarter than everyone else. | I found ways to work smarter and harder than ever. Whenever I wanted to be lazy I asked myself, "Am I working harder than every manager in the country today?" |

The most important lesson I learned is that reversing my Limiting Beliefs took daily action. Reinforcing the Empowering Beliefs became a concrete, actionable plan. When I started to feel nervous or overwhelmed, I knew that there were steps I could take to help myself be the best. It helped remind me that even if I felt like it was out of my hands, it wasn't. Then, when my actions paid off, it reinforced that changing my beliefs had a measurable effect on the outcome.

# LIFE AFTER LIMITING BELIEFS

Once you've reversed Limiting Beliefs and turned them into Empowering Beliefs, it's time to start planning your success. With all the "junk" cleared out, it makes room for all of your potential to shine through. With a fresh mindset and the ability to rid yourself of Limiting Beliefs, you're ready to focus on creating Empowering Beliefs and the life you dream of.

# BREAKING OUT!

What is one big dream you want to accomplish?

_____

What are some specific Limiting Beliefs that are preventing you from accomplishing this dream?

_____

Run each of those Limiting Beliefs through the Limiting Belief framework, and jot down your results here.

Limiting Belief 1

_____

Limiting Belief 2

_____

Limiting Belief 3

_____

Once you eradicate these Limiting Beliefs, what skills and talents are going to be better and stronger?

# NIGHTCAP

## DAY 1: YOUR MINDSET

★ You weren't born to be mediocre - don't let people dumb-down ★
your dreams and expectations

★ Be different, question why some things are the way they ★
are, and rebel when that "why" doesn't make sense

★ Failure means you're making progress. Don't be so afraid of it ★

★ Being different, instead of extremely smart, is often ★
what separates the great from the average

★ Fear is good. It shows you what you need to do ★

★ Limiting & Empowering Beliefs control your actions ★

★ Think unrealistically: When you're too "dumb" to know ★
you can't do something, you'll make it happen

★ Limiting Beliefs can only be limiting if you don't turn them ★
into Empowering Beliefs

★ Be prepared for Limiting Beliefs to creep back in and reverse ★
them again when they do

# DAY 2
## YOUR ACTIONS

# CHAPTER 4

# OUTWORKING THE COMPETITION

## - HUSTLE & GRIT & REFUSING TO QUIT -

*Feeding the outside wood heater last night. Brings back old memories. Seth claims that he "paved the way for Chandler's easy life" but you'll hear about all the work I did at this woodpile during this chapter.*

*12/22/12 - 9:00 am*
*Man it's early! It's Seth's birthday though, and it feels pretty awesome that he's spending it here with me to write the book. I found a big bow in my Mom's Christmas stuff and put it on his head. To see a picture of it, check out his section.*

"Go at something with such dogged determination that you will never ever quit until you see it happen."
- Walt Disney

> ### "The harder I work, the luckier I get."
> ### - Thomas Jefferson

So here we are at one of the most important lessons that I learned from my dad growing up. My dad REALLY knows how to work and man did he teach me how to do the same. Everything he put me through gave me a strong work ethic. That means a commitment to getting a job done well and on time. It also means sticking with a job through difficulties and failures until you get it done right.

Work ethic isn't affected by skill or affluence but by passion and attitude. A good work ethic levels the playing field. Its power allows even the most lackluster performers to get better results than people who are "born stars" but lack social standards. The coveted victory goes not to the one with the most skill, but to the one who works the hardest. It really doesn't matter where you start. If you out-work your competition, you'll come out ahead every time.

Michael Jordan failed to make the cut for his middle school basketball team. The Beatles were told early on by a record label that "guitar groups are on their way out." Tim Tebow was told, "You'll never play Division 1 college football." And yet — they all succeeded! They ignored the naysayers, and they persevered and outworked the competition to make it to the top. It wasn't their initial talent that made them successful; it was their passion and work ethic.

# ATTITUDE IN WORK

My first lesson in work ethic attitude began as a kid on Saturday mornings. My family had an outside wood-burning furnace that required ridiculous amounts of wood to heat our house. As a result, many Saturday mornings I was jarred awake by the miserable sound of a chainsaw outside my window. Hearing my dad use the chainsaw early on Saturday morning made me want to bang my head against the bedpost. It always meant one thing: I'd be outside helping split, load, and unload wood within a half hour. My Dad would come into my room or call my Mom to wake me up and, after stalling as long as possible, I'd make my way out to the woodpile and split wood at a snail's pace. I wanted to make it clear that I didn't enjoy doing it.

My dad would then give me the weekly lecture on my bad attitude and tell me I needed to change it. You've probably heard this speech before. I had too, a thousand times, but nothing changed. I still hated splitting wood and I'd do anything to get out of it!

I got smart and started inviting a friend over on Friday night ... only to have Dad make us both work the next morning. It became a joke amongst my friends: go over to Chandler's house Friday night, and you'll be working on Saturday morning.

---

"Nothing can stop the man with the right mental attitude from achieving his goal; nothing can help the man with the wrong mental attitude."
- Thomas Jefferson

---

"I haven't failed. I've just found 10,000 ways that don't work."
- Thomas Edison

---

During those months of self-pity and whining, I slowly learned my lesson. Amid all the work, I learned the power of attitude. I learned that the work gets done much faster with a good attitude and, as mine changed, so did my output on those Saturday mornings. If I came out to the woodpile with a good frame of mind, I could get much more work done in less time.

The work that I'd hated for so many years became... well, not exactly fun, but I did find it was a good opportunity to strengthen my relationship with my dad. I began to cherish this time with him and used it to ask him questions about business and life. By changing my attitude I not only accomplished way more, but I also was able to learn countless lessons that are helping me achieve my dreams now — and will continue to help me in the future.

## "Change your Attitude, Change your Outcome"

Splitting wood, along with other small challenges I faced growing up, taught me the value of achieving "Mini Successes." My work ethic allowed me to overcome challenges. While I may not have been curing cancer or earning seven figures (yet!), I did start having many small successes that slowly built my confidence and propelled me to take on bigger challenges. I've designed the Breaking Out suggestions in this book to give you Mini Successes that you can build on. We'll talk more about Mini Successes later in the book.

# BREAKING OUT!

## Work ethic
Your ability to consistently get things done well and on-time.

## Attitude
The way you view your circumstances, your goals, and your work.

## How's your work ethic?
On a scale of 1 ("I never get anything done") to 10 ("I'm unbeatable at getting important stuff done well and on-time") ... how would you rate yourself?

1       2       3       4       5       6       7       8       9       10

If you rate yourself less than "10," what's the single biggest problem with your work ethic?

_____

What is one small thing you could change in your work ethic this week?

_____


## How's your attitude?
On a scale of 1 ("I'm negative about everything") to 10 ("I have an extremely positive attitude regarding my circumstances, goals, and work")... how would you rate yourself?

1       2       3       4       5       6       7       8       9       10

If you rate yourself less than "10," what's the single biggest problem with your attitude?

_____

What is one small thing you could change in your attitude this week?

_____

_____

# CHAPTER 5

# DO IT NOW

## - AVOIDING PARALYSIS BY ANALYSIS, AND MY STINT IN REHAB -

When we were outside, Seth and I went out to the "clubhouse" that my dad and I built when I was a kid. My dad doesn't mess around. He even built bunk beds on the inside. Can you tell he's in construction??

### 12/22/12 - 11:12 am
Just tossed around the football with my bro and I'm feeling recharged. But — my fingers are a little tingly. It was pretty cold and Seth was throwing bullets. Don't let the long hair and tight jeans fool you.

I'm going to let you in on a little secret. While still living at home, I had a nasty habit and was forced into rehab. It's not something that I'm proud of, but it's something that still tries to sneak its way into my life.

Hi, my name is Chandler, and I'm a recovering procrastinator. My stint of forced rehab lasted for about a month and was held by my Mom.

She was tired of putting up with my procrastination, and even more tired of having to do the things that I put off.

Our conversations would usually go like this:

Later never came and procrastination rehab began. I came home from school one day to find sticky notes all over the house. They all read *"Do it now"* and were attached to each one of my unfinished projects. I was beyond annoyed, but this tactic actually worked and started me on my journey to killing procrastination.

Procrastination is a form of resistance that keeps us from doing important tasks. It allows us to trick our minds into thinking that we'll *"do it later."* In writing this book, Seth and I made the plans for it during Thanksgiving and will have it written by the end of the year. We're killing procrastination — not using the holidays as an excuse — and finishing the book!

Did you notice anything in that example? Action starts with a plan.

---

## "A dream without a plan is a wish."
### - Herm Edwards

---

## "Half done is undone & done is better than perfection."
### - Adam Carroll

---

# AVOIDING PARALYSIS BY ANALYSIS

A plan will never be perfect. Spending excess time on planning is the mind's way of justifying lack of action. The more time spent trying to make the plan perfect, the less available for putting it to work. Plan the essentials, but the real fun is figuring things out along the way.

## What if I get stuck?

Getting stuck in planning mode is normal! It happens to everyone and it's usually a sign that there are Limiting Beliefs present. Limiting Beliefs create fear and stall all progress. This can take the form of "paralysis by analysis" — which means you are so enmeshed in examining and thinking about a task that you are unable to start working on it. When this point is reached, go back and take inventory of any Limiting Beliefs that still need to be reversed.

---

"When all else fails, clean out a drawer."
- Adam Carroll

---

## What if I'm still stuck?

What do you do when your to-do list is a mile long and you don't know where to get started? You sit there, not knowing where to even get started. The next time you find this happening, go clean out a drawer, organize your desk, or do some other small task that isn't work related. After doing this, you'll have the feeling of accomplishment you need to get started on that long to-do list.

# BREAKING OUT!

## DO IT NOW CHALLENGE

What are things in your life that you need to "Do it now?" Go around your house, office, or bedroom and put "Do it Now" sticky notes on all of your unfinished projects (don't worry about how many there are ... for now, just put a sticky note on each one).

Of everything you attached a sticky note to ... what are the ones you would most like to get off your back?

_____

_____

_____

Over the next week, take care of one task per day. If a task is big, break it down into several smaller chunks. At the end of the week you'll be pretty amazed at the progress you've made.

Make this a daily thing. I don't care if you use sticky notes or paper and tape .... 

# Do it Now!

# CHAPTER 6

# EFFICIENCY

## - MAKING STRAIGHT-A'S WITH ½ THE STUDYING -

*A message from Mom; this is the coffee mug you buy when you raise two rambunctious boys.*

*12/22/12 - 4:00 pm*
*Seth has decided we're going to Puerto Nuevo for his birthday tonight. It's his favorite Mexican restaurant and a hometown treat. With Puerto on the brain it would normally be hard to focus on writing BUT ... this is probably my favorite topic in the whole book.*

## WORK SMARTER - NOT HARDER

My first real job began the summer after my 8th grade year, working for my dad's business. During my first day, I must have heard the phrase *"Make me faster"* from my dad a million times. My one job was to make him as efficient as possible. To do this, I had to be one step ahead of him at all times. I was forced to think ahead and work proactively so that I could anticipate his future needs and solve problems before they occurred.

# "EFFICIENT"
[i'fiSHənt]
Achieving maximum productivity with minimum
wasted effort or expense

Being efficient doesn't mean being busy. Being efficient means accomplishing maximum amount of work with minimum amount of time and effort. By working smarter, you can accomplish more in less time.

Parkinson's law states that: "**A task will swell in proportion to the amount of time that you give yourself to complete it.**" Shorten the amount of time that you have to complete a task and you'll find yourself eliminating pointless distractions in order to make it happen. Removing cell phones, social networking, and all other time-wasters will allow you to clear the clutter and meet your deadline.

In school, I studied half as much as many of my peers and still made better grades on test day. My study habits were born out of laziness: there was only so much studying I could stand, but my parents still expected me to get A's. As a result, I learned how to cut my study time in half, which forced me to study only what was important and in the most efficient way possible. These self-imposed limitations removed any distractions that would send my A.D.D. mind into the clouds.

Here's an example. Let's say you have a short, but important email to draft to your boss, a professor, or a colleague. It shouldn't take you long, but it's a topic you're not familiar with. So you do some online research, but get distracted when a Facebook notification pops up. So you check Facebook. Ten minutes later, you come back to the email. You type out the greeting and the reason for your email. Then you get a text message. You stop to reply, wait for the reply back, and so forth. Five minutes later you get back to the email and get stuck again. Back to the internet you go.

You know the rest of the drill. A task that probably should have taken you about ten minutes total has now stretched into a half an hour — and you're not even done yet!

So what could you have done differently?

First, if you had your research prepared and complete, you wouldn't have needed to refer back to the internet, risking the black hole also known as Facebook. Second, by removing distractions such as your cell phone, you'd be forced to concentrate on the task. Bottom line? Sit down and DO IT NOW.

The best way to improve your efficiency and eliminate minutia is to ask yourself, "What's the fastest way to the finish line (without cutting corners & sacrificing quality?)"

(I learned that last part thanks to an impressive number of speeding tickets!) I ask the question — What's the fastest way to get this done? — several times per day to make sure I'm working smarter instead of harder.

Asking this question does two things: it challenges your mind to be creative and it forces you to continue improving. Coming up with creative solutions makes things fun and it makes problems feel more like opportunities.

Once you've figured out the fastest way to the finish line, you'll be able to enjoy the newfound free time that you have. Being efficient creates this free time and man, does it feel awesome! In one of my best summers ever, I used this technique to create endless free time while making more money than ever before.

It was the summer after my senior year of high school and I decided to run a landscaping and pressure washing business to save up for college. I started with the goal of profiting $5k but doubled it and made $10k by summer's end. I worked smarter by hiring my friends and rewarding them based on how efficiently they worked. I had one rule: only hire people that worked as hard as I did. By doing this, we were able to finish work by lunchtime and spend our afternoons at the lake. I vacationed and had fun all summer, while tripling my income from previous summers.

Now that you've learned about efficiency, here are a few ninja-like efficiency hacks to help you Work Smarter, Not Harder.

## Morning Power Hour

Every morning, as soon as you roll out of bed, dedicate the first hour of your day to uninterrupted action. This means not checking social media, email, or your phone until you've completed your one hour of UNINTERRUPTED ACTION! This action is something that immediately moves you toward the "finish line" (e.g. Prospects closer to signing a deal, term-paper bibliography closer to finished, etc.). It should also be your mostst uncomfortable activity of the day. As you go about your day, your willpower diminishes. Do these uncomfortable actions first while your willpower is the strongest! I recommend that you start by eliminating a few of those "Do it now" sticky notes that you've accumulated since the last chapter.

The best way to make the most of your "Morning Power Hour" is to plan your day the night before. Before you go to bed, write down the most important things you have to get accomplished the next day on a small piece of paper. Keep the paper small to keep the list small. Only write down things that HAVE to be done for you to have a successful day.

## Touch it Once

Whether it's your email, your bills, or your voicemail, only touch it once. Don't read an email if you don't have time to respond. Don't check your voicemail if you can't call the person back. Touch it once — and complete the task! Doing this keeps you from forgetting things, eliminates wasted time, and eliminates accumulation of additional "Do It Now" sticky notes.

## 50 On -- 10 Off

To avoid constant distraction, practice the principle of 50 on, 10 off. For every 1 hour of action (work), spend 50 minutes on uninterrupted action and the last 10 taking a mental break or catching up on email/calls. Do this now, and thank me later.

## Focused Start

How often do you find yourself stuck in looonngg, boring, and unproductive meetings? This efficiency hack is similar to the "Morning Power Hour" but applies to meetings, phone calls, and other business tasks.

You can tell how productive a meeting or call is going to be by what happens in the first 3 minutes. The productivity AND pace are decided within these crucial minutes. If these first minutes aren't handled well, it's almost impossible to turn the meeting around into something productive. Start off a meeting by saying something like "Are you ready to get started?" and get to the point immediately. Tell people right off the bat what the purpose of the meeting is, what the timeframe is, and what needs to get done in that amount of time. Start off your phone calls by saying: "I'm right in the middle of something, how can I help?" or "Heyyy so and so. Whatcha got for me?"

When you start your meetings and calls this way, the people you work with will know that you mean business right away. They'll be impressed by the change of pace and appreciate that you don't want to waste their time. You'll be amazed how much more productive they'll become.

# BREAKING OUT!

## 1/2 TIME CHALLENGE

What are the top 3 things you typically spend the most time on?

_____

Which is the one that you most want to simplify?

_____

How long does this task usually take?

_____

Now — give yourself just half that amount of time to complete the task. Pick something fun to do with the time you saved!

##  BONUS - 80/20 ANALYSIS

What takes 20% of your time but yields 80% of your results?
Spend more time on these activities and eliminate the others that are wasting 80% of your time.

# NIGHTCAP

## DAY 2: YOUR ACTIONS

★ Work ethic is better than natural talent ★

★ Outwork the competition ★

★ Change your attitude, change your outcome ★
creating a good ethic starts here

★ Procrastination – Resistance ★

★ Spend less time planning and more time doing ★

★ When all else fails, clean out a drawer ★

★ Work Smarter, Not Harder ★

★ Being efficient doesn't mean being busy ★

★ What's the fastest way to the finish line? ★

### EFFICIENCY-HACK RECAP
★ Morning Power Hour ★
★ Touch it Once ★
★ 50 on – 10 off ★
★ Focused Start ★

# DAY 3
## YOUR INFLUENCES

# CHAPTER 7

# YOUR INFLUENCES

- SUSTAINING THE CHANGE YOU'RE TRYING TO MAKE -

*12/23/12 - 9:03 am*
*Riddle: What's under-decorated, slightly annoyed, and should never wear a beret?*

*Answer: My brother*

*2nd generation Eagle Scout!... obviously Seth didn't quite make it.*

I once heard that a person can find their income by averaging the incomes of their five closest friends. You are the average of your five closest friends, but in more ways than salary.

They shape you physically, mentally, spiritually, and otherwise. Who are your five closest friends? How do they contribute to who you are?

The people we surround ourselves with have a huge impact on our lives. If you want to know the direction that a person is going in, all you have to do is find out whom they are listening to. The quickest way for someone to change their situation is by changing their friends (influences).

# NEW MINDSETS - OLD FRIENDSHIPS

We've all had them ... the friends who talk us into staying at the party for just an hour more, or convince us to have dessert when we're trying to lose weight. Some friends just aren't good for us.

It can be hard to distance yourself from friends, but if you have a goal and your friends aren't supportive of this goal, they will only drag you down. You can't take new mindsets back into old friendships. This is why an overwhelming number of people that go into rehab for drugs or alcohol end up relapsing. They go back to the same group of friends and expect things to be ok. This applies to us all just as much as it does to addicts. If you experience a mindset shift but take it back to the same group of friends, it will never last.

# INFLUENCED OR INFLUENCING?

At any one point in your life, you're either influencing or being influenced. Every friend that you have either brings you up or takes you down. Good influences help you build momentum while bad influences do everything they can to stop it. If you want to have friends who bring you up rather than take you down, you must become friends with people you aspire to be like.

One spring break, I went backpacking on the Appalachian Trail with my best friend Eli, who I've known since middle school. We rushed to put the trip together and planned to do 30 miles in two days ... not a bad hike. Due to poor planning, the original route was closed. We were delayed by several hours and the new starting point put our destination over 40 miles away. We started our extended hike with no map, overstuffed packs, and with very little daylight left for us to get to our campsite. Off to a great start, right?

The remainder of the trip went about as poorly as it started. We were forced to cover 40 miles of mountainous terrain in two days. Towards the end of the trip, the hiking had taken its toll and every step dealt a dose of some of the worst pain I'd ever felt in my life. I reached my breaking point after topping what I thought was the last mountain climb, only to see another mountain staring back at me. I was pretty crushed. I threw my pack off in frustration and told Eli that I could go no further. Equally frustrated, Eli took a few things from my pack, put them in his and told me that I had no choice but to push through the pain and keep going. He wouldn't let me give up!

That's what real friends do. The best influences are the ones who don't let you stay down when you're at your lowest point. The best influences are the ones who drag you out of your funk and push you (sometimes literally) back to the top.

## A Good Influence

 Challenges you

 Holds you accountable

 Has YOUR best interest in mind

Someone who challenges you will help you build momentum and become a better person. Someone who holds you accountable is not afraid to call you out when you mess up. Someone who has your best interest in mind will give you the advice you need, even if you don't want to hear it. Use these characteristics to ensure that you have the best influences around you. Use them to actively seek out friends and mentors who will push you toward your dreams.

My mentor, James Roper, has all of these characteristics and was one of the major reasons I was able to reach my goal of $100k that summer. He made sure I was always on top of my game and was honest with me when I wasn't.

# BREAKING OUT!

## DO IT NOW CHALLENGE

Write the name of a friend who improves you in each of these ways:

Spiritually

_____

Physically

_____

Mentally

_____

Financially

_____

Socially

_____

Which of these is the area where you need to grow the most?

Call the friend in the area where you need to grow most. Let that person know that he or she helps you in this area of your life, and ask for advice.

If you can't think of a friend who challenges you in one of these areas, seek out a new friend who will!

# CHAPTER 8

# YOUR INFLUENCE

## - LIVING, LEARNING, AND PASSING IT ON! -

*These are the people that showed me that I have influence!*
*I owe them the world.*

*12/23/12 - 11:42 am*
*Just watched a couple videos of a Steve Jobs interview. He talks about bashing into the walls and I have to laugh. I "bash into the walls" so often that I forgot it wasn't normal.*

The most important thing for a person to realize is that we all have influence (including you!). Most of us don't go around proclaiming that because we don't want to appear arrogant or cocky. But the fact is that everyone has some skill at which they excel … therefore everyone has influence in at least one area of their life.

Thinking about the world in this way helps us realize that WE are the ones with the power to change the world and influence others. WE have the power to help others break out of a broken system.

"When you grow up, you tend to get told that the
world is the way it is and your life is just to live your life
inside the world, try not to bash into the walls too much,
try to have a nice family, have fun, save a little money.
That's a very limited life. Life can be much broader,
once you discover one simple fact, and that is
that everything around you that you call life was made
up by people that were no smarter than you. And you can
change it, you can influence it, you can build your own
things that other people can use. Once you learn that,
you'll never be the same again."
- Steve Jobs

# PASSING ON YOUR LEGACY

Helping others break out of a broken system means you can never stop giving. Your influence is your legacy, and your legacy is not yours to keep. Your legacy is for you to pass on to others.

This is exactly what my parents did many years ago. When they met, they were both working at a factory. My dad was a college dropout and my mom was a high school graduate. They were determined to make a better life for Seth and I than the one they had. Then, they shared with us the knowledge that they gained through years of hard work.

Sharing influence with others is a very inspirational process, and it's a two-way street. Initially, our parents inspired us through what they taught us, and as they continued to unveil sections of the Success Map, we continued to grow.

Eventually, we were able to inspire them by showing them the cool new things we were learning and the risks we were taking in order to succeed. The same thing happens when you pour yourself into others. The people you influence will gain confidence through your advice and they will continue to inspire YOU to be better.

# NEVER STOP GIVING
# TO NEVER STOP LEARNING

In order to teach a concept, the teacher is required to understand the information they are teaching on a much deeper level. A large part of understanding something is immersing yourself in it and, whenever possible, getting some practical, real-world experience. This is why doctors have long residencies that consist of supervising and teaching junior doctors. After all, you wouldn't want a doctor teaching future doctors (or operating on you!) who had only ever studied something in class — even if they got an A! The more you teach others, the better you will understand the subject you're teaching.

After running a $100k business and winning Entrepreneur of the Year, I had many aspiring entrepreneurs from the program call and ask for advice. After the first call, I began to think back on my own experience. It was through this reflection that I learned even more about myself, the mistakes I had made, and the things I needed to change going forward. Since then, I've had the opportunity to train other students to start their own business just like I did. As good as it feels learning things for yourself, it feels even better teaching these things to others.

You don't have to be rich or super successful to use your experiences to help someone else. If you'd like to use your own experiences to help others, there are plenty of potential opportunities. Here are some ideas:

★ Ask local churches if any members have needs — it could be as simple as driving someone to a doctor's appointment or church, or helping someone prepare for a job interview.

★ Ask school counselors if anyone needs help tutoring in a subject you excel at. You may also ask if any teachers feel their students would be interested in hearing you speak about your job.

★ It doesn't always have to be professional help, either. Ask staff at a retirement home if any residents would appreciate being read to or having someone simply spend time with them.

★ Check organizations in your field of employment or study. Does anyone need a mentor?

★ Think outside the box. For example, are you good at keeping calm in stressful situations? Domestic violence or homeless shelters are always looking for individuals to help in crisis situations, or assist clients in looking for work or housing.

Once you realize that you have the power to influence others through your actions, you'll never be the same again.

It's at this point that you can decide to make your mark and change the people around you for the better. By helping them break out of a broken system, you're inspiring the next generation of innovators and leaving your legacy for generations to come. This is what it means to Never Stop Giving.

---

*12/23/12 - 11:30 pm*
*Made it to the beach last night after a 4 hour drive and a pit stop for Seth to get Christmas presents (such a slacker). I looked for food while he was getting presents but not many places were open this close to the holidays! While browsing, I had a chance encounter with a friend. Got to catch up with him and then finish out the drive.*

---

# BREAKING OUT!

What great thing(s) do you want to be remembered for?

_____

_____

As important as it is to have positive influences in your life, it is equally as beneficial to be a positive influence for someone else. List three people in your life who you feel could use some encouragement or advice. How can you positively influence them this week?

_____

_____

★       ★       ★

# NIGHTCAP

## DAY 3: YOUR INFLUENCES

★ You're the average of your five closest friends in ★
salary, personality, and smarts

★ You can't take new mindsets into old friendships ★

★ The quickest way to change your situation is by changing your friends ★

★ Become friends with people you aspire to be ★

★ Everyone has influence ★

★ The people you influence will inspire YOU to be better ★

★ Teaching is learning ★

# DAY 4
## YOUR MOMENTUM

# CHAPTER 9

# MANY MINI SUCCESSES
## - GROWING THROUGH FORCED OPPORTUNITIES -

---

*12/24/12 - 9:05 am*
*Rise and shine, it's Christmas Eve! We're writing these chapters much faster than when we started! This outline-writing method is really working and I can honestly say that this is the first time that I haven't seen an outline as a waste of time. Now I see what all those English teachers were talking about. Starting to write but being tempted by the smell of the muffins that Mom is cooking ....*

---

"Perseverance is not a long race;
it is many short races one after another."
- Walter Elliott

---

A few years ago, I learned how to ride a snowboard. By that, I mean I slid down the icy mountain on my butt. I must have fallen a hundred times that day but I kept getting back up and trying again. At the end of the day I was moving like an 80 year old with arthritis, but I felt like a champ. I had plenty of bumps and bruises but I left with one thing I didn't show up with — a little more confidence in my snowboarding ability.

Every time I fell down that mountain, I was presented with a new challenge — a new opportunity to get back up and ride better. Each time I got back up was an opportunity for a Mini Success.

We get these chances daily but many of us miss them because they're often disguised as roadblocks. When we look at each roadblock as simply a pain in the you-know-what, we might miss the lesson we have to learn from it. Solving problems and overcoming challenges provides us with the opportunity to learn what not to do in the future and also teaches us that we have the ability to move through obstacles.

Try to change your mindset about challenges, failures, and roadblocks. Your mindset determines whether they are setbacks or whether they help catapult you to the next level of success.

## FAILURE ⇨ EXPERIENCE ⇨ PROGRESS ⇨ SUCCESS

I was unaware of it while I was growing up, but my parents were giving me countless opportunities for failure and the inevitable Mini Successes that followed. It wasn't until I interviewed my parents in preparing to write this book that I understood this concept. Sports, scouts, school, music, and work around the house, all presented opportunities for many Mini Successes.

Mini Successes are where all momentum begins. As I built a strong foundation of Mini Successes, it was much harder for failures to bring me down. It wasn't the skills from Mini Successes that propelled me past these failures; it was the newfound confidence that I gained in myself that allowed me to overcome them!

> *Muffin break. Mmmm — Still warm! Writing and eating.*

# TAKING CONSISTENT ACTION

In 1911, there were two teams of adventurers that set out on a 1,400 mile journey to become the first people in modern history to reach the South Pole. One team made it out alive and the other died trying.

The first team stuck to what they called a "20 mile march." This meant that no matter the weather or their energy level, they would hike 20 miles each day. The other team took a completely different approach.

On days with great weather, they would push themselves and do as many miles as possible. On days with bad weather, however, they would hunker down with little to no progress. Can you guess which team made it back alive and which team died trying? You're right — the "20 mile march" team made it out alive.

# GOAL SETTING

Do you know the best way to practice the 20 mile march? It's by consistently setting goals. I know what you're thinking: *"Oh NO... not another lecture on goals."*

Nope. I'm just going to show you how goal setting has been responsible for some of my biggest successes. When I first started my internship with Student Painters, I had a lofty goal of running a $130,000+ business (a company record) and becoming the *Entrepreneur of the Year*. The thing is, I had no idea what I needed to do in order to hit that goal.

That's when my mentor sat me down and we started breaking down the goals for my business. This was just the beginning. After the first goal setting session, we continued to make goals throughout the preseason (selling and marketing time before summer) and throughout the summer. We made all kinds of goals: weekend goals, weekly goals, monthly goals, etc.

It was these small goals that helped me reach my big goals of $100,000 (my modified goal) and *Entrepreneur of the Year*. I hope you caught the side lesson there. It's ok to modify your goals as you go along!

You can't possibly anticipate every roadblock or change of course you'll encounter as you work toward your goal. Sticking to a goal that isn't realistic is only going to cause anxiety and disappointment. If at any point you feel like your goal is unattainable, reevaluate it and set a new one that is reachable but challenging. Setting this new goal will revitalize you and give you something to work toward that you feel you can actually achieve.

When making goals, it's important to make them SMART goals.

| **S** | **M** | **A** | **R** | **T** |
|-------|-------|-------|-------|-------|
| SPECIFIC | MEASURABLE | ACHIEVABLE | REALISTIC | TIME BOUND |

The biggest mistake people make when setting goals is not following the criteria above. They make broad, unrealistic goals that are very generalized, can't be measured, and have no time limit.

If you make goals that are missing any of these characteristics, you're giving yourself an easy way out. Any grey area around your goals is a way to let yourself off the hook and make excuses for why they weren't accomplished.

# DEALING WITH FAILURE

As you attempt to build Mini Successes, you will probably fail early and often. Failure is a good thing. Failure means you're trying new things and moving forward. It's when you fail that you learn and grow the most. It's sort of a paradox, but the better you are at failing, the more you will succeed.

Dealing with failure is difficult, and the way we deal with it has a direct impact on our ability to fail forward. Failing forward means that you accept the failure, while looking for the ways it will teach you a lesson and propel you closer to your goal. Your mindset will determine if you fail forward or if you allow failure to hinder your progress. Embrace it, knowing that it brings you one step closer to where you need to be!

Learning to snowboard was a pretty embarrassing process and I failed many times. As humbling as it was, I learned a heck of a lot faster than if I would have sat on my butt all day in the safety of the ski lodge. Now I'm flying down the mountain and teaching friends how to do the same.

---

"I can accept failure. Everyone fails at something.
But I can't accept not trying."
- Michael Jordan

---

"Excuses are an indication of a lack of desire."
- Dane Maxwell, Co-founder of The Foundation

---

# BREAKING OUT!

## FORCED OPPORTUNITIES

Think of two things that you want to learn this week (or do for the first time). Choose two things that are outside your comfort zone and are new and exciting!

If you need help thinking of something, reference the list below:

★ Learn to cook a new dish

★ Try a new exercise class

★ Hit the gym

★ Go skydiving

★ Go deep sea fishing

★ Camp out

★ Hand-make a picture frame for a favorite photo or award

Now go do those two things this week. No excuses!

## FORCED FAILURE

Make it your goal to fail at something. In other words, choose to do something that you KNOW will bring you at least one failure this week.

# CHAPTER 10

# BE PREPARED

## - ADOPTING AN EAGLE SCOUT MENTALITY -

*This is me getting the "Manager/Entrepreneur of the Year" award from Young Entrepreneurs Across America. All that hard work paid off! I love cruises — but I love them even more when they're free (paid for by the company).*

*12/24/12 - 11:12 am*
*Finished off my breakfast and Mom and Dad just left for a bike ride so it's much more quiet here now. I'll be able to focus a lot better. My A.D.D. brain just couldn't focus with all that noise. Now if I could get Seth to stop playing music ....*

## GETTING DRAFTED

Success is on the horizon and the next phase of your life will determine if you achieve it. To get to this point, you've built a strong foundation of Mini Successes. Opportunity has come your way, and you're taking advantage of it by taking action. Getting to this phase is just like getting drafted into the minor leagues in baseball.

After being drafted, some players spend years playing in the minor leagues and never make it to the majors, while others advance quickly. The toughest part of the uncertainty phase is not knowing if you'll make it. It's the not knowing that wears on you, allows Limiting Beliefs to creep back in, and makes you question if you'll ever make it. This is what happened to me during my middle-of-the-summer struggle with my painting business.

To climb your way out of this uncertainty phase, you'll have to do what I did: reverse Limiting Beliefs as quickly as they come up and continue to take action. If Limiting Beliefs are not dealt with immediately, they'll cause you to doubt yourself and you'll regress by throwing in the towel and stopping inches short of your goal. Taking action and reversing Limiting Beliefs will allow you to keep moving forward, even when it gets hard.

# BE PREPARED

That's the Boy Scout motto. I became an Eagle Scout in high school, and the road to becoming an Eagle Scout is all about being prepared. It's about building skills to prepare for whatever life throws your way.

There's a saying, "Expect the best, but prepare for the worst." Essentially, being prepared means thinking ahead and trying to anticipate what could happen ... not just what you expect will happen. Challenge yourself to do this in your planning and goal-setting process. The more you do it, the more you'll acquire the flexibility and adaptability that will help you respond quickly and avoid disaster when plans go awry. Also, the more you do it, the better you'll get at "looking around corners" in your long-range planning.

You can often avoid serious trouble when things don't go as planned by being proactive rather than reactive. I'll talk a little more about this in the next chapter.

---

"Many of life's failures are people who did not realize how close they were to success when they gave up."
- Thomas A. Edison

---

# CONQUERING FINAL OBSTACLES

When I was running my painting business, I ran into some serious problems halfway through my summer that almost broke me. They broke my spirits and almost allowed me to settle for average. I was on a small weekend vacation trying to take a break when all hell broke loose for my business. I got a call from my production manager informing me that he, along with half of my crew, were quitting. Wow! Talk about a vacation spoiler!

We'd had three weeks of ridiculous rain (the rainiest summer since the 1950's) and the guys hadn't been able to work much so they were looking for other work. I now faced being three weeks behind schedule with only half of my crew working. I knew that I would continue to get behind schedule if I didn't hire more people immediately. This was a daunting task, and for the first time ever, I thought that I might not reach my goals of Entrepreneur of the Year and a $100k business.

After a couple days of wallowing in my own self-pity, I decided that there was no way I would let this break me. After doing countless interviews, I brought out ten people to a paint training that I held by myself. I picked a couple of the best candidates from this training and formed a team of all-stars. The new recruits, working with my existing team, went on to paint a ton of houses and helped me reach both of my goals for the summer. They were constantly impressing homeowners with how quickly and efficiently they painted.

On the path to success, there will always be roadblocks that seem insurmountable. Often, these roadblocks are the final obstacles in the way of success, but they keep most people from achieving their dreams. The old saying, "When the going gets tough, the tough get going," definitely applies here.

**As an entrepreneur, "no" is when I get started.** When someone tells me that I can't do something or that it's not possible, I start working even harder to make it happen. This is one characteristic that all entrepreneurs have; they're problem solvers. Getting a "no" motivates them to try harder and pull out all the stops. Even if you don't consider yourself an entrepreneur, moving past "no" is super important for conquering final obstacles that come up.

Looking back on my business, I realize that this was one of the first big challenges that I faced. By using the confidence and skills I had built up over years of running small businesses, I was able to overcome this challenge and many others on my journey to becoming Entrepreneur of the Year.

Final roadblocks like these are tipping points. Approach them with newfound confidence and Empowering Beliefs, conquer them, and you'll be able to add them to your list of Many Mini Successes.

# BREAKING OUT!

What are two times in your life when unexpected events/obstacles caused problems for you or stopped your progress?

_____

_____

In each case, looking back, how could you have been prepared, even partially, to better handle the unexpected?

_____

_____

In each case, how did these unexpected obstacles teach you a valuable lesson, or help bring you closer to your goal?

_____

# CHAPTER 11

# THE DISCIPLINE TO "DO"

## - WHY I'M DEAD-BROKE IN THE MIRROR -

*12/24/12 - 2:31 pm*
*Seth and I stepped outside for some fresh air, a Subway™*
*sandwich, and a view of the beach. Apparently, not too*
*many people go to the beach the week of Christmas. It*
*was pretty relaxing but now we're back at it.*

## SUCCESS IS HERE

You've made it to the major leagues. You've got your signing bonus, your fancy new uniforms, and even a little paparazzi, but you haven't played in a single game. Those final obstacles that you had to overcome seem trivial when looking back at them now. Your wildest dreams have come true but you're as nervous as ever because you have officially been noticed.

Sometimes one of the biggest obstacles is our own fear of actually succeeding (crazy but true). This sometimes comes back to being afraid of failure in the end. Other times, it can be related to deeply rooted Limiting Beliefs, such as the fear of being more successful than your parents.

# BUILDING DISCIPLINE

Ironically, reaching success often brings a new level of resistance that you may not have faced before. Having achieved something important, it's easy to lose momentum, lose focus, and just coast. If you've given yourself a "well-deserved rest" after achieving a milestone, but can't get fired up about your next goal or project, then this is a sign that complacency is creeping in.

Remember the saying, "Make a plan. Work the Plan?" Now, more than ever, it's important that you continue to work the plan by building the Discipline to Do.

The Discipline to Do requires you to make tough choices every day, and it isn't easy. These tough daily choices are exactly why you see so many more people in the gym during the first week of January than the rest of the year. Setting a goal is the easy part - it's following through that gets tough.

Here are some tips for rebuilding the Discipline to Do if you feel you've lost momentum:

★ Review your life dreams. What are you trying to accomplish, and why?

★ Revisit your goals. Remind yourself that each one is a tangible, critical step along the path to the successful life you're trying to build.

★ Check your beliefs. Have Limiting Beliefs crept back into the picture and begun to slow or stop your progress?

★ Enlist the help of your influencers. Nobody succeeds alone. We all need people who are in our corner when we need encouragement, motivation, information, and mentoring. Seek out the people who can help you get back on track.

# PROACTIVE VS. REACTIVE

Building discipline starts with the Morning Power Hour, as described in Chapter 6. Every morning we wake up, we can start our day in one of two ways; proactive mode or reactive mode. Most people wake up in reactive mode because it's so easy to do!

You roll over in bed and grab your phone to check Twitter, Instagram, or email and you instantly start REACTING to everything the world is sending your way. I've found for myself that after I start a day in reactive mode, it is SOOOOO HARD to switch over to proactive mode and sometimes it never happens.

Look at the mornings of most successful people (especially entrepreneurs) and you'll see that their mornings are sacred. They start their day in proactive mode and focus on doing some of their toughest tasks first. I want you to do the same! If you use your Morning Power Hour and start your day in proactive mode, it will be so much easier to keep the discipline you've worked so hard to create.

---

"Every morning, before I put on my suit,
I look at myself in the mirror as if I'm dead broke.
Then I go out and make something of myself."
- Michael Porcaro, Owner and founder of Tides Enterprises

---

# KEEPING DISCIPLINE

People ask Seth and I all the time to tell them about our "big break" and that's really impossible to answer. Our early success came from our initial work but our "big break" came only when we kept the Discipline to Do beyond the early success.

The internship that helped me start my painting company awards a cruise to the top 20% of students who run a $55k business or larger. When I hit this goal, James (my mentor) told me that another intern had said the following: "Chandler made the cruise already?

Why doesn't he just wrap up his business and take the rest of the summer off? That's what I'd do. I'd stop." Although making the cruise was exciting, there was no way that I would give up the discipline that got me there! I looked at myself in the mirror every morning as if I hadn't hit $55k so that I would keep moving towards my goal of $100k.

---

"If you're bored with life – you don't get up every morning with a burning desire to do things – you don't have enough goals."
- Lou Holtz

*12/24/12 – 7:30 pm*
*Finished up for the day and took a walk on the beach with my Mom. We saw some dolphins, played football with some kids, and found this cool work of art that someone made.*

*Tomorrow is Christmas. Hope Santa brings something good!*

# BREAKING OUT!

## MORNING MIRROR CHALLENGE

Starting tomorrow, look at yourself in the mirror each morning as if you've accomplished nothing. Go out that day and accomplish something worth talking about.

(Consider a Do It Now sticky note on the bathroom mirror until this becomes a habit for you.)

What habits do you have that are largely REactive? Do you obsessively check Facebook? Watch too much TV? Identify three things in your daily life that are reactive and list an alternative, PROactive activity.

_____

_____

_____

_____

# NIGHTCAP

## DAY 4: YOUR MOMENTUM

★ Mini Successes are Opportunities disguised as challenges ★
Gain confidence by giving yourself more opportunities for Mini Successes

★ Practice the "20 mile march" by making S.M.A.R.T goals ★

★ The better you are at failing, the more you'll succeed ★

★ Final obstacles are tipping points, with success waiting on the other ★
side. Push forward through the uncertainty

★ It's tough to gain success, but even tougher to keep it ★

★ The Discipline to Do separates the stars from the overnight successes ★

★ There's no "big break" ★

★ Start your day in proactive mode: protect your morning ★

★ Look at yourself in the mirror each morning as if you're dead broke ★

# DAY 5
## MERRY CHRISTMAS!

*Seth & I love Christmas so much we decided to dress up! Costume-less, we improvised with bed sheet super hero capes! As you can see, this was a much needed break.*

*(We're losing our minds from all this writing!)*

# DAY 6
# YOUR MONEY

---

*Many people never learn how to manage their money and feel as if they're trapped by it. Schools don't teach students about money and most parents don't either. But how can parents teach their kids about money if they never received a financial education themselves? If it weren't for my parents who taught me these vital skills, I'd still be clueless about money and it would have control over my life. The coming chapters will teach you about money — how to take control of it and make it work for you.*

# GIVING

## - THE BOOMERANG EFFECT -

*12/26/12 - 9:12 am*
*Christmas was awesome! My parents got me a golden ticket for the Succeed Faster conference in Chicago this summer. I went last summer and it changed my life. What an awesome gift! Couldn't be a better time to write about giving.*

## MORE BLESSED TO GIVE

As I'm writing this, the concept of giving and the joy that it brings is fresh in my mind because Christmas was just a day ago. Have you ever noticed the jolly spirit that surrounds the holidays? Why is everyone so happy? They're happy because they go out of their way to give to others. Giving a gift brings true happiness to the soul. It's more of a blessing to give than to receive and it's amazing how much happiness comes from giving.

I was talking with my friend Jess and she said, "It's amazing to me how your parents make money just so they can give it away." My parents have always been this way, and I'd like to share a few things they taught me about giving. Giving to others is not something that can wait until you "make it." Giving to others should be a part of your everyday life, regardless of the size of your income.

---

"We were designed to be rivers, not lakes. Our gifts should flow through us to others, rather than being held in us like a reservoir." - Dad

---

Growing up, I would always tell myself that I want to make a ton of money so I could give to others and help those in need. I told this to myself for years, just like you probably do now. One day, I was challenged by my mom to stop and ask myself, "What are you doing NOW to give to others?" The answer was, "Not much."

I had tricked myself into thinking that I would make a bunch of money first, and give to others second. I realized through this conversation with my mom that this giving philosophy was backward. She told me that "Any time I make money the #1 priority, it never comes ... but the second I make giving #1, the money comes faster than I know what to do with it." This shows through her real estate career. The more she focuses on serving and giving to others, the more houses she sells. After this conversation, I thought to myself, If I'm not doing much to help others now, how can I expect to magically flip the giving switch when I'm "rich"?

# GROWING BY GIVING

Investing in the growth of others is what leads to your own personal growth. Ask my parents and they'll tell you that their greatest success comes from their giving. Giving has always been the number one priority for them, even when they barely had anything to give.

When preparing for the book, my Mom shared the following about giving:

"Sometimes you give money, time, love, a hug, a listening ear, a meal, or an encouraging word that goes a long way. Give something!

Notice the little things around you. I noticed that a neighbor's grass needed cutting. I went over to cut it, only to find out that he was depressed due to the death of his wife. So I mowed his grass and invited him to family dinners and he began to love again! It's not always about money, but about time and love."

Seth and I decided to write this book while at a family dinner — and this man (Mr. Silas) was there! He's a part of the family now.

My mom has taught me that when you focus your time and attention and energy on giving to others, you always end up being able to give them something they need.

From my mom, "Consider a mother who has carried a handicapped child for seven years everywhere she walks. Just by giving your time on a mission trip, you meet her and can give her money to buy a stroller that she could not afford. You could literally lighten her load."

*My mom took this picture moments after they gave this woman the stroller.*

My mom is definitely one of the most selfless people I know and she is constantly focusing on how to help others. She taught me the importance of showing compassion for those around me and taking the time to make them feel special. This is SO EASY to do and yet nobody does it!

Greet people with a smile, ask them about their day, say thank you, or compliment someone on the clothes they're wearing.

This is the most basic form of giving and it doesn't even cost anything. It might just be the thing that will turn someone's day around. How awesome does it feel when you get a compliment? Really awesome, right? I've given a compliment to someone and then heard days later from that person's friend how much it brightened their day. Give people compliments. You never know when it might brighten their day.

The next chapters in the section on money will show you how to grow your income, protect your income, and give it away. Money is power; the more money you make, the more power you will have to bless others through GIVING.

# BREAKING OUT!

## THE GIVING CHALLENGE

Show a random act of kindness by helping someone, without them knowing, for nothing in return.

For example:

★ Pay for the person behind you in the drive-thru.

★ Leave a gas or grocery gift-card in the mailbox of a neighbor (Maybe put the person's name on it, so they won't worry that it's there by mistake).

★ Tidy up a family member's (or neighbor's) yard when you know they're at work and won't see you.

# CHAPTER 13

# THE DEBT TRAP

## - HOW TO GET OUT AND STAY OUT -

*12/26/12 - 10:21 am*
*Really liking this cabin! It's really peaceful out here and it's been great being able to write distraction-free. Too bad it's too cold to jump in the lake BUT ... there's a pretty awesome looking hot tub. Definitely using that tonight!*

As I entered college, I saw many people around me falling into a trap. Everyone around me had accepted the fact that they'd be taking on massive amounts of student loans to pay for school. This was really shocking to me because being anti-debt had been drilled into my head my entire life. My parents would never let me go into debt and only allowed me to buy something once I'd saved up the money. I feared debt and thought that this fear was universal. But I realized that it is scarce and people have no problem burying themselves in debt for the rest of their lives.

## "DEBT"
[dĕt]

*n.* An obligation or liability to pay or
render something to someone else

# AVOIDING THE TRAP

People all around me (in college) were selling off future freedom for current debt. The thing that really shocked me was hearing friends talk about graduating with upwards of $40k in debt. Some even said that they didn't know how they were going to get the money to finish school. For many, college is the first step toward building a mountain of debt that will be incredibly difficult to overcome.

It's almost always possible to prevent or minimize debt. In this case, for example, you can save a lot of money by going to community college for two years, and then transferring to a 4-year college and finishing up with the same bachelor's degree.

Some people take a "gap year" in which they work full-time, live at home, and save almost every dollar they make. In a year or two, they have enough to pay for four years of college.

It's also possible to save a lot of money by commuting to a nearby college or university. This isn't for everybody, but if you have a decent relationship with your parents and are willing to immerse yourself in campus life — to be sure you get the full college experience even though you don't live in the dorms — you can have a great four years, get your degree, and come through with no debt when you graduate.

# FREEDOM VS. ENTRAPMENT

The pathway of debt leads in two different directions. Freedom from debt is Empowering. Entrapment by debt is Limiting. Lack of debt builds momentum, while having debt makes for an uphill climb.

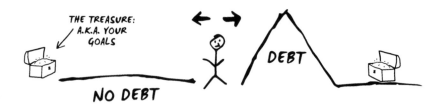

THE TREASURE:
A.K.A. YOUR GOALS

NO DEBT

DEBT

# DEBT KILLS FREEDOM

Remember learning about indentured servants in history class? They had no freedom because they were owned by their debt. As soon as they could work off their debt, they could be free. The most important thing to me is my freedom, and that can't be bought, not even for a billion dollars.

DEBT KILLS FREEDOM

FINANCIALLY        GEOGRAPHICALLY        VOCATIONALLY
$                                              J.O.B.

Having large amounts of debt when you graduate college forces you to immediately get a crappy job that you don't want in order to make payments on the loans that you took out. This keeps you from having the freedom to move where you want, hold out for your dream job, or take any type of "financial risk." You are forced to get and keep a job because payments are due. It is debt that forces you to get the job, and debt that forces you to keep it.

# TAKE CONTROL OF YOUR DEBT

If you already have debt, assess the situation and figure out how you can most quickly and efficiently minimize it. If you need financial advice or guidance, seek that out. Ask people you respect, "Who do you know that's knowledgeable about managing credit, debt, and money matters?" See if you can find a trustworthy friend, relative, co-worker, teacher, or neighbor who is knowledgeable about personal finances.

Share your debt situation with that person and ask for advice. Better yet … ask several people! If you're having trouble finding someone who can help, go to BoltBros.com, find our contact info, send us an email, and we'll personally do what we can to help you get out of the trap that is debt.

If you already have loans but are still in school, you can do what my friend Josh did. Here's his story:

A year and half into school Josh was faced with a tough choice: continue going to school and rack up more debt or take a year off to work and save up money. Neither scenario was appealing.

With over $10k in loans, he knew that going deeper in debt wasn't an option, but he didn't want to delay graduation.

So what did he do? He hustled. Despite the fact that he thought he wouldn't qualify for most scholarships, he worked his butt off and applied for everything he could get his hands on. He didn't take no for an answer.

After a couple of months of hard work he was given a financial aid package worth over $18,000 a year for every year until he graduates. They actually write him a check for over $2,000 per semester that he can use for housing, food, etc.

Now that school is covered, he's working and using his money to pay off his $10,000 debt and is on track to graduate debt-free.

Once you begin to take control of your debt, you will see financial, geographical, and vocational freedom enter back into your life.

If you are lucky enough not to have debt yet, good for you! Be sure to become knowledgeable and get good advice before taking on any debt in the future. Know what you're getting into, and understand the implications on your future freedoms and options.

# BREAKING OUT!

If there were a magic wand that could remove all debt from your life, what would that allow you to do:

Financially?_____

Vocationally?_____

Geographically?_____

Socially?_____

What's a first step you can take this week toward eliminating that debt and unlocking those freedoms?

# CHAPTER 14

# THE 4 PILLARS OF STEWARDSHIP

## - HOW TO STOP BLEEDING CASH -

*My mom clipped a lot of coupons and she eventually decided to put them into a binder. Naturally, I found a ridiculous picture for her cover. It always gets a good laugh.*

*12/26/12 - 11:45 am*
*Just finished outlining this chapter and I've got so much to cover here. My parents really taught this well. I'm over on the couch laughing as I think of all the stories I could tell. Which ones do I choose??*

The story of my parents is a pretty remarkable one. When my brother was young, my parents were struggling to get by on low paying jobs, but were doing the best they could. Three weeks before Christmas, my dad was fired and forced to go into business on his own in order to provide for his family.

It was at this point that he vowed to make something of himself so that our family would never be put in that situation again. It's amazing looking back at the progress they've made. They've never made large amounts of money, but they've done all they can to take care of what they have. Through their actions, they've taught the principles of stewardship that are outlined in this chapter.

## "STEWARDSHIP"
### noun ['stü-ərd-'ship]
The conducting, supervising, or managing of something; especially: the careful and responsible management of something entrusted to one's care

Stewardship is one skill that is as rare as a two-dollar bill. It turns upside down the notion that making more money means having more money. With stewardship, the amount of money you make is irrelevant; it's how much you keep that matters!

Like work ethic, stewardship levels the playing field. It allows someone who gets paid $30k/year to keep as much money as someone who gets paid $100k/year. The difference in take-home pay is determined by the way a person manages expenses. Although raising your income is great, managing your expenses is what determines how much of it is really YOURS. Income can be controlled in the long run but expenses can be altered immediately. Start changing your spending habits today, and you'll see the benefits tomorrow.

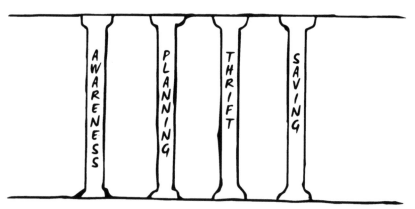

# 4 PILLARS OF STEWARDSHIP

## Awareness
In order to begin managing your money well, you must first become aware of the ways that you are spending it. This seems like a simple step, but it can yield some of the most shocking discoveries. There are many ways to monitor past expenses, but I recommend setting up a mint. com account. It takes about 5 minutes and shows past expenses on credit cards, debit cards, mortgages, and more.

It also generates a report of where your money is going — food, entertainment, bills, etc. This will help you easily identify where you can cut back on unnecessary spending.

## Planning
Now that you're aware of the ways you're bleeding cash, you can set forth a plan to cut future expenses. Whether you've used one or not, it's never too late to dust off the old-fashioned budget.

Envelope Trick: There are endless ways of doing this online or on paper, but sometimes it's best to use the envelope trick.

Make 4 envelopes for: Saving, Giving, Spending, and Investing. Break this down weekly and put money in each envelope accordingly. Tracking your progress weekly allows you to monitor your progress frequently and make changes to your spending.

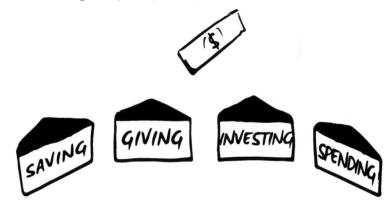

## Thrift
This is the big one! From coupon clipping to having basic TV (free), my Mom taught me how to be thrifty and get creative. Being thrifty means eliminating wasteful expenses and stretching your dollars further. The majority of a person's paycheck is spent $5-$10 dollars at a time, and from morning coffee to lunch out, there are endless ways to trim these expenses.

Another ninja-like thrift tactic is eliminating unnecessary monthly expenses. Monthly expenses drain your bank account and many of them can be eliminated or reduced without a painful shift in lifestyle.

## Saving
The final stage of stewardship involves saving the surpluses of money that you've created after following the previous steps. There's no minimum here. Saving little amounts at a time may seem trivial, but it's the first movement towards progress. Use this newfound savings to pay off debt or to invest. Either way you use it, you're one step closer to making your money work for you!

# BREAKING OUT!

## BUDGET CHALLENGE

Set up an account at mint.com.
Find the top 3 things you spend your money on.

_____

_____

_____

What are some ways you can reduce or eliminate those expenses?

_____

_____

_____

Now make a budget for the upcoming month and stick to it!

# CHAPTER 15

# LEARNING THE RULES

- THINK LIKE A BUSINESS OWNER BEFORE YOU BECOME ONE -

*I know it looks like a "selfie" but Seth took this picture while we were on a break back at home. This is the dump truck that I used to load mulch and pine straw back in my landscaping days.*

*12/26/12 - 2:05 am*
*Seth made some awesome chili for lunch. Then we realized that we're pretty much out of food. It looks like we're going to try and find a place to eat dinner tonight in this tiny town!*

In middle school, I remember reading the book *Rich Dad, Poor Dad* by Robert T. Kiyosaki. This was the first book I'd ever read about money and it rocked my world. This book is all about learning the rules of the game of money. Knowing the rules is the only way to win the game, but the rules are never taught.

For the many who are not taught these rules, this becomes a Limiting Belief. Reverse this belief into an Empowering Belief and you now have the power to take charge of your financial education, regardless of your background. To get you started, I'll share a few money tips and tricks.

# TYPES OF INCOME

There are 3 types of income: earned income, investment income, and business income.

## Earned Income

If you're like most Americans, you make your money through earned income by trading hours for dollars. The frustrating part is that Uncle Sam snatches up roughly 50% of this income.

## Investment Income

Revenues from CD's, bonds, stocks, and mutual funds are considered investment income. This income is taxed at a lower level than earned income, but a higher level than business income.

## Business Income

This includes revenues from rental properties and businesses that you own. This type of income is taxed less than any other income, in addition to the benefits gained from owning your own business.

# STARTING YOUR BUSINESS

Not only can starting a business be a revenue generator, it can also be a great way to save money on your taxes. I started my first "business" when I was a kid attending Scout camp in the summer. My mom sent me to camp loaded with snacks and my first business idea was born. I began selling and trading my snacks and amassed a small fortune. I came home with awesome knives, money, and a ton of other cool stuff. This was a simple start towards building my own business.

From there I ran the "Papa Poncho's" canteen at my school and made $2k in three months. I was pretty excited about getting paid to go to school. Next up was the landscaping and lawn care business. I ran that business one high school summer to earn $10k towards college. The following year I ran the over-$100K painting company and made over $17k to once again put towards my college expenses.

Notice a pattern here? My first business wasn't a smash hit but I continued to build on my Mini Successes to run bigger businesses each time. With each new success, I placed a new block on my foundation of Many Mini Successes. This is exactly what I want you to do.

Whether you're in college working for beer money, in the real world working for rent money, or anywhere in between, you can start building a small business that will put money in your pocket. No business is too small!

# BUSINESS TAX SAVINGS

There are SO many ways that you can save money by starting a business! Even if you never make a dime from the business, starting YOU, Inc. will be the best financial move you ever make. You can create an LLC for a couple hundred dollars and instantly become a business owner. Starting the business will allow you to instantly pay less in taxes and make back the $200 you paid for the LLC. You can do this by writing off some expenses as business expenses.

Having a business (that shows intent of earning profit) is the best way to save tax dollars. This allows you to write off business purchases that can also be used for personal use such as a lawnmower, cell phone, part of your utilities for a home office, or an SUV/truck with a payload of 6000+ lbs.

When I go to a conference, travel for business, or even buy supplies such as ink for my printer, these are considered business expenses and therefore write-offs on my taxes. Here's one more money-saving technique: if you own the *"non-residential"* building your business is in, you can pay rent to yourself and use the rent expense as a write-off on your taxes.

Here's some other non-business related tax write-offs that you might not know about:

★ Depreciation of assets — write off the depreciation (the reduction in the value of an asset with the passage of time) of your home, car, etc.

★ Charitable Donations

★ Mortgage Interest

★ Medical Bills — ONLY if they add up to a certain percentage of your income

If you're unsure of what items can be written off, be sure to consult an expert — a tax attorney or accountant.

# YOUR BUSINESS DOESN'T HAVE TO BE PROFITABLE

You're probably thinking: "Doesn't my business have to make money for it to make sense for me?" The answer to this question is no. Having a business that loses money is a tax write-off. You can use the losses from this business as savings on your taxes.

The only way to break out of the broken system of money is to learn the rules and tricks of the game. If you don't know the rules, you can't play the game. There are many more money tricks and tips, but these are a few of the basics.

# BREAKING OUT!

## CREATE YOU, INC!

Find a simple business idea and incorporate yourself, whether for revenue or for tax benefits. List some business ideas and the potential write-offs you'll be able to take advantage of.

**BUSINESS IDEAS**          **POTENTIAL WRITE-OFFS**

_____

_____

_____

*We're shooting off some fireworks tonight to celebrate finishing up the book!*

# NIGHTCAP

## DAY 5: YOUR MONEY

★ You can't magically flip the "giving switch" when you're rich ★
Giving should be a part of your life regardless of the size of your income

★ Our gifts should flow through us like rivers rather ★
than being stagnant within us

★ If nothing else, give compliments or a smile to those around you ★

★ Random acts of kindness make the world go round ★

★ Debt Kills Freedom: Financially, Geographically, Vocationally ★

★ Find someone you trust and have them take an outsider's look ★
at your finances. Reach out to us if you can't find someone!

★ Making more money doesn't mean having more ★

★ Income can be controlled in the long run but spending habits ★
can be changed immediately

# 4 PILLARS OF STEWARDSHIP

## AWARENESS
Figure out where you're bleeding cash by setting up a mint account

## PLANNING
Put together a plan to cut future expenses (envelope trick)

## THRIFT
Find ways to trim expenses. The majority of your paycheck is spent $5-$10 at a time

## SAVING
Save your extra money and use it to eliminate debt or take a trip

★ Business income is taxed less than any other types of income ★ (earned or investment income)

★ Starting a business is beneficial, even if its not profitable ★

★ Start a business today, no matter how small. The worst thing that can ★ happen is you'll save some money on your taxes

# DAY 7

---

## BRINGING
## IT FULL CIRCLE

*Taken from a mountaintop apple orchard down the road. As you can tell, we're pretty exhausted after this sleep-deprived and Adderall-filled week of writing. Not exactly our best snapshot of the week.*

*12/27/12 - 9:48 am*
*Seth & I had a great talk last night in the hot tub about how awesome this experience has been. This week has flown by! For one more time, we're putting ourselves on the clock. We need to write this conclusion and pack before it's time to check out of the cabin!*

# RESISTANCE TO INDIFFERENCE

We've covered a lot of ground on our journey. Now you too have the Success Map that our parents gave us many years ago. It's up to you to take it and use it. The mediocre life path that so many people follow is obviously broken!

If you begin using the map that we've given you, you'll start to build a resistance to indifference and you'll unlock amazing things within your own life. Going with the flow and being average is no fun! Be different.

The minute that you understand that you can poke life and
something will pop out the other side, that you can change it,
you can mold it. That's maybe the most important thing. It's to
shake off this erroneous notion that life is there and you're just
gonna live in it, versus embrace it, change it, improve it, make
your mark upon it. I think that's very important and however
you learn that, once you learn it, you'll want to change life and
make it better, cause it's kind of messed up, in a lot of ways.
Once you learn that, you'll never be the same again."
                    - Steve Jobs

# SUCCESS MAP RECAP

## Mindsets

Mindsets are where it all begins. Changing your mindsets will change
the way you see the world. Start by reversing those long held Limiting
Beliefs that are holding you back from dreaming big and taking action
towards your dreams. Mindsets tie into each part of the Success Map.
At each point in the map, there will be mindsets that need to be shifted;
this is expected. Continue to shift mindsets and reverse Limiting Beliefs
throughout the journey.

## Actions

A change in action is required for a change in mindset to stick. Before
you act, Make a Plan. Once you've made the plan, it's time to "Do it Now"
and Work the Plan.

## Influence

Changes in mindset require a change in influence. You can't take new
mindsets back to old influences. At any one point in time, you are
either influencing or being influenced. Who's influencing you? Who are
you influencing? Surround yourself with people that will grow your
mindsets and then share your mindsets with others. Leave your legacy
and inspire others.

## Momentum

We talked about the 3 stages of momentum, but everyone starts at
level 1. Which stage of momentum are you in? Building momentum is a
direct effect of the action that you take.

Advancing through the stages of momentum requires constructing a foundation of Mini Successes, building the Discipline to Do and keeping it!

## Money

Your money will lag 12 months behind your mindset. Your mindsets may be changing, but you won't see the results from these changes until 12 months later. Many of the things that were taught in this book will take little time to implement but you'll have to wait to see the results. Be patient and don't get discouraged because this is typical. The only place you will see quick results is by implementing the money tricks and tips.

By using the Success Map that was outlined in this book, my brother and I have had success in two completely different industries: music and business. Using the tools that I was given by my parents has allowed me to have more fun and enjoy more success than most people my age. Now that you have the tools, it's up to you to go out and use them. I continue to use them every day to grow and succeed at a higher level.

# WHAT I'VE LEARNED

Writing this book over the past seven days has been an incredible journey for me. I hope your journey in reading it has been equally incredible. I never thought that I'd write a book, and it feels surreal to be writing the last chapter. I've gained an even greater respect for my parents over the past seven days and it's been fun working with my brother on this project. We grew up a decade apart, but were able to create many memories together through this experience. Writing this book was a Mini Success!

Over the last year, I've mentored other college and high school students. I've also spoken to these groups about ways that they can better their lives.

Writing this book has brought me so much joy and has been incredibly rewarding. It has also helped me realize just how fired up I get about helping other people achieve their dreams. Not only has it renewed my commitment to furthering my own business goals, but it has also solidified that I want to continue mentoring, coaching, and speaking to groups across the country.

If any part of this book helped you, I'd love to hear about it. Drop me a line at chandler_bolt@yahoo.com.

Thanks for taking this journey with us! I hope you've enjoyed it and have been challenged to better yourself and the people around you. You've also taken your first giving step by supporting an awesome charity with your book purchase.

Go out and "Do it Now!" This is your reckoning time.

Chandler Bolt

_____

# THE SPEAKING ENGAGEMENTS

## TUNNEL VISION & THE ART OF GETTING WHAT YOU WANT

**How do you gain the confidence to start a $100,000+ business at 18 years old while managing employees that are all older than you?**

By the end of this eye-opening presentation, you'll learn how to get what you want by:

★ Learning to say "NO"... Even when it's tough to do.

★ Using Tunnel Vision and blocking out what's unimportant.

★ Building confidence through Many Mini Successes.

This talk is not just for aspiring entrepreneurs.

In "The Art of Getting What YOU Want", Chandler uses real life case studies to show how he used these techniques and:

★ Went from non-starter & Mr. Irrelevant ... to #1 on the tennis team in less than a year.

★ Became a drumming wiz and started traveling with a band within 2 years of picking up drumsticks.

★ Started and ran businesses with over $300,000 in revenue by age 20.

## THE POWER OF PEOPLE

This session is all about how to connect with people that will propel YOU forward.

And NO ... I don't mean by attending a "networking event" and peddling your business cards with a smile and a handshake.

This interactive keynote will teach your organization how to get in with anyone, anywhere, anytime ... AND ... how to get them to WORK WITH YOU.

The program can be delivered as a keynote, breakout session, or half-day workshop. It's best for sales companies, college students, entrepreneurs, and anyone looking to boost their bottom line through The Power of People.

# GETTING THINGS DONE IN HALF THE TIME

### Are you tired of working LOOOONNGGG hours with little to show for it at the end of each day?

Chandler expands on lessons from his book "The Productive Person" and addresses how to manage the ultimate challenge ... work-life balance.

He also breaks down the most helpful tips and tricks from the book, giving the audience actionable techniques and real-world examples that they can INSTANTLY apply in their lives.

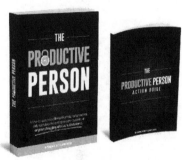

In this talk, you'll learn:

★ How to stop wasting time and Work Smarter, NOT Harder.

★ 4 Efficiency Hacks and how they can keep you from wasting 2+ hours PER DAY!

★ How to delegate, eliminate and liberate yourself from the clutter of everyday life.

★ To create more time to do what you love by outsourcing your worries & frustration.

Whether you're an over-stressed student, over-worked employee, or an entrepreneur, you'll walk away from this talk with the knowledge and plan you need to be more productive and take back your free time while still getting things done.

## THIS TALK IS FOR YOU

For more information, contact chandler_bolt@yahoo.com

# THE PEOPLE

★

## WHO BROUGHT THIS BOOK TOGETHER

Writing a book is one thing — finding and correcting 5000+ spelling errors (mainly Chandler's) and errant commas (mainly Seth's) is a much harder job! The following people are the all-stars that took our manuscripts from shabby word documents most language arts teachers would scoff at into one cohesive masterpiece master's thesis.

Thank you all for pouring countless hours (and your hearts and souls) into editing, proofreading, formatting, internet research, fact-checking, suggestion-making, and going of the extra mile at every turn to make this book great!

### LYNNE BOLT HANSEN ★ NANCY ZIEGLER

### KRISTINA BRUNE ★ IDA FIA SVENINGSSON

### SUE QUENVILLE ★ NATHAN HAINES

### JESS PITSCH ★ ZACK DUNN ★ JOSH KOZIC

### TYLER WAGNER ★ JAMES ROPER

### ADAM CARROL ★ MITCH MATTHEWS

**ART DIRECTORS**
Ida Fia Sveningsson & Seth Bolt

**PHOTO CREDITS**
Selfies out of necessity: *Seth & Chandler Bolt* - Photo of Chandler (The Why) & #Behindthescenes photos: *Steve Brown* - Stamps: *Jessie Parks* - USA map: *Sam Fisher* - Chickens: *Ana Roa Szwarcberg* - PMI & NEEDTOBREATHE photo: *Joshua Drake* - Stick drawings: *Seth Bolt*

**ADDITIONAL PHOTOGRAPHY**
Ryan Morrison, Jess Pitsch, Larry Bolt and Regina Bolt

# THE DEDICATION

Two of the most amazing, hard working, loyal,
faithful, funny, & disciplined parents in the world.

Regina & Larry Bolt

WE LOVE OUR MAMA!

WE WROTE THE BOOK ON BLACK CONSTRUCTION PAPER

BOLT BROS WITH GENERAL ELECTRIC CEO JACK WELCH. HE'S A BIG FAN OF OURS

★

# THE OUTTAKES

CHIEF SLAPPING BASS - SETH WAS BORN WITH A HEAD FULL OF HAIR

#BEHINDTHESCENESOFMAKINGTHEBOOK

CHANDLER BOLT,
LADIES MAN SINCE AGE 4

SETH MORTIFIED BY HIS MOM'S NEW PERM

EAGLE SCOUT IN
TRAINING WITH
THE ROYAL RANGER
THAT TAUGHT HIM
EVERYTHING →

THE ROYAL RANGER →

EAGLE SCOUT ↓

THE FAM
BACKSTAGE AT A
NEEDTOBREATHE
CONCERT ♪♫

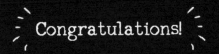

## Congratulations!

You just read a book and saved a life! That's something to brag about! Please tell your friends & followers about our book and our cause. This is not just another book; it's a mission to help people, and it's a way you can multiply goodness in the world!

---

# SHARE!

---

We believe the debt we owe our parents is one we can never repay. We are blessed richly because of their investment in us, and the best thing we can do is pay it forward by sharing their wisdom with others and by investing in others. We wrote this book to do just that: to help people and to help PMI save lives. But we cannot do this without your help in spreading the word on a grass-roots level. We need your "word-of-mouth!" Will you join us by sharing this with your friends??

**GIFT THIS BOOK!**

1 BOOK = 1 LIFE

**TELL YOUR FRIENDS!**

#1Book1Life

**CONTACT US** about buying books in bulk for classrooms, book clubs, & study groups.

breakingoutbooks @gmail.com

# URGENT PLEA!

Every book sale purchases a life-saving malaria pill.
Here is a simple, but powerful way you can help us keep
these smiles alive!

★ ★ ★ ★ ★

# REVIEW

We really appreciate all of your feedback, and we love hearing
what you have to say.

We need your input to make the next version better, and we need
5-star reviews to help sell more books.

Please leave us a helpful REVIEW on Amazon.

## Thanks so much!
### - Seth & Chandler -

# NANCY ZIEGLER
Editor + all-star human being

As a toddler, Nancy Ziegler's first words were probably, "Let me help you clarify that." She is, at heart, a communicator. By day a training and communications strategist ... by night an avid reader of many genres ... Nancy's primary work includes crafting high-impact solutions for a variety of business and entrepreneurial needs. She works with large corporations to help create engaging learning experiences for internal audiences... as well as with authors and speakers to help frame, organize, and articulate their messages. Her work with Seth and Chandler Bolt has been immensely satisfying - and one heck of a fun ride!

## ZIEGLER TRAINING INC.
Email: nancy@zieglertraininginc.com

★

# HIRE THESE
## TALENTED PEOPLE TO WORK FOR YOU!

# IDA FIA SVENINGSSON
Formatting and typesetting of this book, cover design, logo design and website design for www.boltbros.com & www.sethbolt.me

Everything Ida touches turns to creative gold. Hailing from her motherland, Sweden, Ida often works internationally with clients to create custom designs that focus on connectivity and high level visibility, while also maintaining the flexibility to fit the plethora of social media platforms and online pathways clients use to connect to their audience. Her creations embody the heart and soul of your project and "jump off the page" into the hearts of your viewers. An avid music lover and multi-talented workaholic, when Ida's not launching brands, she's photographing bands! Protecting her sanity is her horse, Krummi, which she rides every day.

## IF DESIGN
Email: info@idafiasveningsson.se
Website: www.idafiasveningsson.se

# ★ ★ ★ ★ THE ★ ★ ★ ★
# LAUNCH TEAM

| | |
|---|---|
| **Adrienne Long**<br>West Union, SC | **Caitlin Sweeney**<br>Brooklyn, NY |
| **Alex Lytle**<br>Florence, KY | **Caitlyn Behmlander**<br>Kennesaw, GA |
| **Allee Mixon**<br>Springfield, MO | **Chelsea Lyssand**<br>Charleston, SC |
| **Alyssa Watson**<br>Clemson, SC | **Chelsea Miller**<br>Huntington, WV |
| **Amanda Brannon**<br>Winder, GA | **Christina Hutchison**<br>San Luis Obispo, CA |
| **Amanda Coop**<br>Memphis, TN | **Christina Remie**<br>Amherst, MA |
| **Amanda Crisp**<br>Portsmouth, NH | **Daniel Gilstrap**<br>Cleveland, GA |
| **Anne Pellettieri**<br>Chicago, IL | **Daniel Goodman**<br>Boiling Springs, NC |
| **Arielle Bacon**<br>Chesapeake,VA | **Danielle White**<br>Grand Rapids, MI |
| **Ashley Eure**<br>Orange County, CA | **Dennis Sutherby**<br>MI |
| **Ashlyn Gathman**<br>Plainfield, IL | **Emily Moffitt**<br>Kansas City, MO |
| **Ashley Webb**<br>Lubbock, TX | **Emily Rivet**<br>Atlanta, GA |
| **Brianne Valdez**<br>Sheboygan, WI | **Erin Godwin**<br>Annapolis, MD |

**Heather McDougle**
Charleston, SC

**Kristy Spencer**
Boise, ID

**Holly Wright**
Mt Eden, KY

**Lauren Rovensky**
Seattle, WA

**Hunter Freeman**
Clemson, SC

**Linda Jackson**
Hermosa Beach, CA

**Ida Fia Sveningsson**
Sjöbo, Sweden

**Lonnie Barker**
Houston, TX

**Jayne Hendry**
Somerville, MA

**Lora Nation**
Versailles, KY

**Jen Badger**
Bagley, IA

**Maggie McDaniel**
Mascoutah, IL

**Jenna Higgins**
Birmingham, AL

**Mandy Gilstrap**
Cleveland, GA

**Jenna Jahnke**
Saginaw, MI

**Maria Stevenson**
Nashville, TN

**Jennifer Bennett**
Dallas, Texas

**Marti Deacon**
Matthews, NC

**Jennifer Burt**
Charleston, SC

**Mary-Anne Gillis**
Fairfax, VA

**Josefin Steding Selander**
Glasgow, United Kingdom

**Matthew Ruiz**
Houston, TX

**Kaitlin Graff**
Burnsville, MN

**Megan Cleland**
Poland, OH

**Kaitlin Wilke**
Sheboygan, WI

**Megan Owens**
Walhalla, SC

**Kayla Hardin**
Okeechobee, Fl

**Melissa Krimmel**
Tampa, Fl

**Kelsey Kufner**
Brillion, WI

**Michelle Harrison**
Morristown, NJ

**Kristy Kay Scarborough**
Jacksonville Beach, FL

**Nikita Stephens**
Greeneville, TN

**Patrick Palmer**
New Brunswick, Canada

**Pete Dueckmann**
Lemgo, Germany

**Pete Ford**
Traverse City, MI

**Rachael Cleland**
Poland, OH

**Randi Marie Owens**
Walhalla, SC

**Raquel Reyna**
San Diego, CA

**Rebecca Groh**
Waynesboro, VA

**Rebecca McClain**
Morristown, TN

**Reyna Brizuela**
Houston, TX

**Robin Young**
Glasgow, United Kingdom

**RosePearl Vazquez**
Macon, GA

**Samantha Walker**
Anna, IL

**Sarah Tehan**
Quincy, MA

**Shanna Dee Gilbert**
Pella, IA

**Shannon Sullivan**
Charleston, SC

**Shayla Gordon**
Owings Mills, MD

**Shauna Young**
St. Louis, MO

**Shelbi Meisch**
Kansas City, KS

**Sue Parrish Duda**
Joliet, IL

**Tori Davis**
Madisonville, TN

**Torri Lawrence**
Flint, MI

**Tyler Blount**
Lawton, OK

**Whitney B. Ray**
Winston-Salem, NC

**Windy A. Bailey**
Las Vegas, NV

52802178R00130

Made in the USA
Charleston, SC
22 February 2016